BULLS, BEARS, AND MASSACRES

BULLS, BEARS, AND MASSACRES

A Proven Method for Investing in the Stock Market

William J. Diamond

Lifetime Learning Publications
A division of Wadsworth, Inc.
Belmont, California

London, Singapore, Sydney
Toronto, Mexico City

Developmental Editor: Lorraine Anderson
Designer: Donna Davis
Jacket Designer: Benedict Norbert Wong
Illustrator: John Foster
Composition: Dharma Press

Printed in the United States of America

1 2 3 4 5 6 7 8 9 10–86 85 84 83 82

This publication is designed to provide the author's opinion in regard to the subject matter covered. It is sold with the understanding that neither the publisher nor the author is engaged in rendering legal, financial, or other professional services. If legal or financial advice or other expert assistance is required, the services of a competent professional should be sought.

The author specifically disclaims any personal liability for loss or risk incurred as a consequence of the use and application, either directly or indirectly, of any advice or information presented herein.

Library of Congress Cataloging in Publication Data

Diamond, William J., 1919–
Bulls, bears, and massacres.

Includes index.
1. Investments—United States—Handbooks, manuals, etc. 2. Stocks—United States—Handbooks, manuals, etc. I. Title.
HG4921.D49 332.63'22'0202 82-66
ISBN 0-534-97945-9 AACR2

Table of CONTENTS

List of CASE HISTORIES

PREFACE

For many years I have been using and refining a system for buying and selling low- and medium-priced stocks on the New York and American exchanges. As a result, my net worth has grown steadily year by year. In return for my investment of eight or so hours of time every week, I have had the satisfaction of feeling that I am the master of my own destiny, making investment decisions that have been sound for the most part, based on objective criteria that have been easy to calculate and apply. I wrote this book to teach my system to individuals such as physicians, dentists, lawyers, engineers and business persons who have had no formal training in investment methods and have only a limited amount of time to devote to the management of their capital.

You will notice that I have deliberately avoided the use of superlatives like "best" and "easiest" in describing my system. I make only modest claims for it. I feel it is a disservice to imply, as so many books do, that there exists some magic formula for certain success in the stock market. There is no such magic formula. As is the case in most human endeavor, the ultimate secret of successful investing is *hard work*. All I claim for my system is that it is relatively simple to learn, requires diligence but not brilliance to apply, removes some of the emotional uncertainty that can make investing so wracking at times, and can be applied with expectation of at least modest success.

I also do not claim that the elements of my system are new. Most of them are not. Aside from the Index of Merit, they have been known for many years. What is new, however, is the way I have integrated the elements into a total system. This book is primarily written for investors who have a history of little or no success in investing in the stock market. Obviously, if you have been buying and selling on the advice of your broker and have been making a profit acceptable to you, you should continue to rely on such advice. If you have been investing in a fund that has been successful, you should stick with it. Even the successful investor, however, can benefit from applying the system described in this book in conjunction with his or her present system.

What This Book Requires of You

In order to benefit from reading this book, you should have some familiarity with the procedures and terminology of stock market investment. If you are new at it, you can pick up the required knowledge by reading one of the primers listed in the back of this book in Appendix B. Many brokers offer copies of such primers to new customers.

You should own an inexpensive hand-held calculator to speed up the arithmetic you will need to do. This book is based on accepted mathematical principles and formulas that you need not understand to apply effectively.

You should have a small amount of capital to invest, at least $5000 but less than $25,000. My system will work for the investor with a larger amount of capital, say up to $250,000, but for simplicity's sake I direct my discussion toward the smaller investor. If you do have more to invest, simply take my recommendations and buy more shares, or buy higher-priced stocks, or include more stocks in your portfolio.

You should have a broker you trust to do your buying and selling and supplying of information. You should also have a genuine interest in learning more about the workings of the market and the behavior of individual stocks in different situations. You should have the fortitude to stick to the system even when some brokers, tipsters, and advisory services are giving out contrary advice, because the system only works if you use it.

You should have a subscription to the *Wall Street Journal* and *Barron's*, and you should enjoy reading them faithfully.

Up-to-date information is essential to making the system work. Obviously, keeping up with this information is going to take some time. To really benefit from this system you must be willing and able to devote about sixteen hours to setting the system up and at least four hours a week thereafter to keeping it running.

Last but perhaps most essential, you must have the intention and the self-discipline to commit yourself to applying this system diligently on a long-term basis. If you aren't interested enough to truly want to keep at it, it's not going to work for you. Sporadic efforts will not pay off. Remember, I didn't promise you would get rich quick with little or no effort. What I can claim is the following.

What This Book Will Give You

When you have finished reading this book and following the instructions contained herein, you will have the same working system that I have used successfully for years. You will have the framework for accumulating a portfolio of stocks and for buying and selling profitably so that your net worth will grow year by year at a satisfactory rate. And you will have the sense of confidence and security that understanding the fundamentals of such a system brings.

I wish you well in your investment endeavors.

William J. Diamond

Part I

THE SYSTEM

Chapter 1

PREMISES OF THIS SYSTEM

Every system for playing the stock market is based on a set of premises, whether explicit or implicit. In this chapter I will discuss

- the premises upon which this system is based
- the essential elements of this system, and how they are derived from its premises

The Premises

The premises upon which this system is based are as follows:

1. The objective of the investor is to make a consistent profit in the stock market over the long term.

2. Future stock prices cannot be *predicted* by external indexes or by stock market averages.
3. In order to make money in the stock market you need not be able to *predict* the bottom of a bear market or the top of a bull market, but only to *identify* when such a market has ended.
4. The Dow Jones Industrial Average and the American Exchange Market Value Index are reliable indicators of the *present state* of the exchanges they monitor.
5. The stock market obeys the financial version of the second law of motion in physics.
6. The prices of individual stocks stop declining at approximately the same time as market averages stop declining, and stop advancing at approximately the same time as market averages stop advancing.
7. Individual stocks are at most times either overpriced or underpriced.
8. Owning a diverse portfolio of stocks is desirable.

Discussion of the Premises

Premise 1. Although making money is properly the primary objective of everyone who invests in the stock market, that objective can be arrived at in a variety of different ways, to fit the investor's needs. Some investors want to make a quick killing and are willing to take enormous risks in the hope of doing so. Other investors hope to provide fixed incomes for themselves by buying stable, high dividend stocks and holding on to them forever. Some are not as concerned with dividends as with the possibility of long-term capital gains. And so on.

This system is designed to enable one to show a consistent

profit on short-term trading. Short-term trading is defined as buying and selling any one stock as often as once every two months or as infrequently as once every two years, depending on the behavior of the stock and market conditions. Consistent profit means that you should not expect to show a profit on every transaction, but over the long haul your profits will exceed your losses so that your net worth will grow.

Premise 2. The perfect index to *predict* the future of the stock market or individual stocks does not exist, nor will it ever exist. This is because it is impossible to predict the stock market's behavior. Nevertheless, many investment systems attempt to base predictions on external indicators such as the money supply, the index of leading economic indicators, the inflation index, car sales, the interest rate, the production index, ad infinitum. Many attempt to base predictions on stock market averages or stock market indexes such as odd lot sales, short sales, advance-decline ratios, volume of sales, and so on.

The point is that while these indicators do an adequate job of measuring the present or past state of the economy, the present or past state of the market, and the present or past mood of investors, they are not a sound basis for making *predictions* about the future. For example, if interest rates have been going up for the past two months, this is bad for most stocks in most situations, and might explain why stock prices have gone down the last two months. But it does not enable one to predict that interest rates will continue to increase over the next month and thereby cause a drop of forty points in the Dow. While it is wise for an investor to be aware of and sensitive to these indicators, it is not wise to base investment decisions on the supposition that the indicators have a cause-and-effect relationship with the market.

The most telling argument against external indicators is that they have failed to predict correctly in many cases. Those indicators that predicted a bull market in 1977 were absolutely wrong; the NYSE was in a bear market throughout 1977.

Those indicators that predicted a bear market were also wrong; the Amex was in a bull market throughout 1977.

Premise 3. In order to make money in short-term trading one must buy low and sell high. This does not mean that one must buy at the exact bottom of the market and sell at the exact top. Many investors define happiness as buying a stock at 10, selling at 20, and watching it drop to 10. They define gloom as buying a stock at 10, selling it at 20, and then watching it rise to 30. While it can be psychologically very rewarding to buy at the bottom and sell at the top, it is *not* a prerequisite for success.

This system is based on the premise that if you can *reliably* identify when a bull market or a bear market has ended, shortly after the fact, you can make sound investment decisions that will pay off in the long run. As said before, you must not expect to make a lot of money fast. There is an old saying: Bulls can make money in the market; bears can make money in the market; pigs never make money in the market.

Premise 4. As noted in Premise 2, stock market averages cannot *predict* future stock prices. What they can do is reliably indicate the effect of the factors that are influencing the price of stocks on the exchange they monitor *at the moment*. This is an important distinction, and one that you should bear in mind.

In this system, the Dow Jones Industrial Average has proven an adequate indicator of the present state of the New York Stock Exchange (NYSE). As you may know, the Dow is the total price of thirty stocks traded on the NYSE, corrected for splits, etc. The stocks are those of large stable industrial companies that have been in business for many years. The stocks are usually high in price and are traded in large volumes every day, so that the total dollar volume of these stocks traded each day is a substantial part (25 percent) of the total dollar volume traded on the NYSE on any day. The theory behind the Dow is that the movement of a majority of stocks on the NYSE will in general be indicated by the movement of this sample of thirty stocks.

Of course, on a day-to-day basis individual stocks will move in any direction they want to, regardless of the Dow. On a specific day, the Dow might go up five points, but typically only 900 of the stocks traded on the NYSE will end up higher in price than on the previous day, and maybe 500 will actually decrease in price, while 350 will remain unchanged. The Dow is not a good monitor for the lower-priced stocks traded there; the American Exchange Market Value Index is a much better monitor of such stocks.

There are some students of the market who argue that the NYSE Industrial Average or the Standard & Poor's (S&P) 500 Average are better market indicators than the Dow. Still, over time the Dow has proven to be a reliable enough indicator to provide a basis for one of the elements of this system. If its quirks are also taken into account, as they are in this system, it can be a source of valuable information. And the same goes for the American Exchange (Amex) Market Value Index. It is a good monitor of the movement of stock prices on the Amex, and of lower-priced stocks on the NYSE.

Premise 5. The stock market obeys the financial version of the second law of motion in physics. This law states that a body in motion will remain in motion without change in speed or direction until acted upon by an outside force. For example, when you fire a gun toward the sky, the bullet leaves the gun because of the explosive force of the gunpowder, which starts it in an upward direction. Unless some other force interferes, the bullet will continue upward forever. Eventually, the force of gravity interferes and prevails, and the bullet stops its upward motion and starts downward. Again, the bullet continues to fall until it is acted upon by an outside force, the resistance of the earth when it finally strikes the ground.

Applied to the stock market, this law means that when due to a number of financial, political, human, and other factors, the price of most stocks are going up, they will continue to go up until these conditions are moderated or reversed. Then the market average will start down and will continue to go down until the conditions are again reversed. The mass of the market is so great that once it is started upward, it will continue to move upward for long periods of time. A great force is required to stop a great mass. The same thing applies when the market is going down. The force required to stop a bear market must be great and usually takes a long time to develop.

Premise 6. What is the relationship between prices of individual stocks and market averages? As noted above under Premise 4, on a day-to-day basis individual stocks move in any direction they want to, regardless of the average monitoring the exchange. But in order to build a system, we need to be able to generalize, and then build in flexibility to make allowances for those stocks that do not move with the market.

By definition, the end of a bear market is when the prices of most stocks stop declining. If you can identify that a bear market has ended, you can reasonably expect that a majority of the stocks on that market are low priced and that the market will begin to move upward and that a majority of the stocks on that market will probably increase in price. Likewise, bull markets always end and they are always followed by bear markets. At the end of a bull market the prices of most stocks are high, and you can reasonably expect that most will probably decrease in price.

Premise 7. Though the price of stock in a company varies from day to day, the intrinsic value of the company most certainly does not change from day to day in the same way. Thus it stands to reason that there must be some true, fair, or correct value for stock in any company. As the price of a stock decreases, it must either be getting closer to a fair price or becoming more underpriced. Likewise, as the price of a stock increases, it must be getting closer to a fair price or becoming overpriced. The above is true even though one does not know the value of this fair price.

The fair price of a stock depends upon such factors as book value, present and potential future earnings, quality of company management, company assets, nature of the business, sales and sales increases. A stock should be bought when it is underpriced and sold when it is overpriced.

Premise 8. It follows that since the prices of most but not all stocks will rise or fall along with the market average, it is not a good idea for an investor to put all his or her eggs in one basket. There is nothing earth-shattering about this; it is common wisdom and has been incorporated into this system.

The Elements of This System

From the above premises, a list of required elements of a good system can be derived. First, from Premise 1, if you are to show a long-term profit on short-term trading, you must have a system that provides you with simple, clear indications of when to buy and sell stocks without incurring excessive risk and at prices that in the long run earn you profits. From Premise 2, such a system cannot require that you make *predictions* based on averages or indexes.

From Premise 3, the system should enable you to reliably identify when a bear market is in progress and when it has ended, and when a bull market is in progress and when it has ended. From Premise 4, the system can rely on the Dow Jones Industrial Average and the American Exchange Market Value Index to represent reasonably accurately the present and past state of the market. From Premise 5, a statistic calculated from the above must measure the direction of the forces that are influencing these markets.

From Premise 6, if you are aware of the present direction

of the market, you can also be fairly confident that you have a good idea of the present direction of individual stock prices. If they are downward, you should not be buying any stock. If they are upward, the system should provide you with reliable answers to the question, "When is an individual stock overpriced, and when is it underpriced?" The system should give you some clear and simple index to tell you at what price to buy and at what price to sell.

Finally, from Premises 7 and 8, the system should help you choose a diversified portfolio of reasonably good stocks from which to buy and sell.

So, in summary, a good system should provide:

- a simple, clear way to identify when a bear market is in progress and when it has ended
- a simple, clear way to tell when a bull market is in progress and when it has ended
- a simple, clear way to recognize signs that the market may be in for a massacre
- a simple, clear way to tell when a reasonably good stock is underpriced during a bull market
- a simple, clear way to tell when a reasonably good stock is overpriced during a bull market
- simple, clear instructions for making objective buy and sell decisions based on this data

Chapter 2
HOW THE SYSTEM WORKS

Now that you are familiar with the premises of this system and the necessary elements derived from those premises, it's time for a brief preview of how the system works. Subsequent chapters will take up each of the elements of the system in greater detail. This chapter discusses

- the materials you will need to get the system started
- the specific procedures that make up the system

Materials You Will Need

Since making good decisions is greatly facilitated by having good information available on which to base those decisions, much of this system is devoted to the collection of data. You will need a way to keep track of the data you will be collecting. You should buy yourself the following items if you don't already have them around the house:

- a three-ring binder
- binder paper
- three-hole graph paper
- divider tabs
- colored pencils
- a hole punch
- a ruler

As mentioned in the preface, you should also have a hand-held calculator and a subscription to the *Wall Street Journal* and *Barron's*. With all these items in hand, you will be ready to get started.

Identifying Bull Markets, Bear Markets, and Massacres

The first part of the system gives you a simple, clear way to tell when bull and bear markets are in progress and when they have ended, and a way to recognize signs that a massacre may be impending. The procedure used for identifying bull and bear markets is called *moving averages*. Using simple arithmetic that can be done very quickly on your calculator, you will produce a moving averages table and chart for each of the exchanges, the NYSE and the Amex. The use of this procedure is described in detail in Chapter 3.

Chapters 4 and 5 give you detailed instructions for interpreting the data you've been shown how to collect in Chapter 3. By following these instructions you should be able to recognize the signs that a bear market is in progress or is ending, and that a bull market is in progress or is ending.

Chapter 6 shows you how to construct *trend lines* on a daily market chart and the moving averages chart to alert you to approaching sudden fluctuations or reversals in the market.

Selecting Reasonable Stocks to Buy and Sell

The second part of the system gives you a simple, clear way to tell when reasonably good stocks are overpriced or underpriced during bull markets. The first step for you to take is to select a reservoir of reasonably good stocks about which to collect data. Chapter 7 tells you how to do this. You will be shown how to keep a data sheet and a chart on each stock in your reservoir, to be updated periodically.

Then Chapter 8 tells you how to use this data to calculate what is called the *Index of Merit* for each stock. Again using simple mathematics that can be done quickly on your calculator, you will arrive at a figure that will tell you whether the particular stock is overpriced or underpriced. You are told how to look at trend lines for individual stocks to time your transactions. Finally, Chapter 9 tells you how to make use of all this data you have collected on the state of the market and of individual stocks. Specific instructions are given for basing your buying and selling decisions on the objective data you have collected and interpreted.

Throughout the book detailed case histories are provided to demonstrate this system in practice. These are provided only to enhance your understanding of the application of the procedures described. They are not to be considered as proofs of the system or indicative of the way the market can be expected to behave, because the market's behavior is absolutely unpredictable.

Related Investment Considerations

As you may have gathered, selling everything is advised when you have reliably established the end of a bull market, and buying nothing is advised while a bear market is in progress. This leaves your money uninvested for a time, so in Chapter 10 U.S. Treasury bonds and notes are discussed as one possible place for you to park it. Chapter 11 discusses a way for you to think about investing to produce a steady income for yourself in retirement.

In summary, the book covers the elements of the system in this order:

- *Chapter 3*: how to chart moving averages for the NYSE and the Amex
- *Chapter 4*: how to interpret your charted data to identify bear markets in progress and the ends of bear markets
- *Chapter 5*: how to interpret your charted data to recognize bull markets in progress and the ends of bull markets
- *Chapter 6*: how to collect data on the daily pulse of the market and construct trend lines on a chart, to alert you to possible massacres ahead
- *Chapter 7*: how to select a reservoir of reasonably good stocks and how to collect essential data on them
- *Chapter 8*: how to calculate the Index of Merit on each stock and to determine whether the stock is overpriced or underpriced; how to construct and interpret trend lines for individual stocks
- *Chapter 9*: how to make objective decisions to buy and sell from your portfolio based on the data you've collected
- *Chapters 10 and 11*: related investment considerations

Part II

THE MARKET

Chapter 3

CHARTING MARKET AVERAGES

While the Dow Jones Industrial Average and the American Exchange Market Value Index are reliable indicators of the present state of the exchanges they monitor (as stated in the premises), only a statistic calculated from them can provide truly useful information for you. In this chapter you learn how to calculate this statistic, called a moving average.

This chapter shows:

- why moving averages are more reliable indicators of the trend of the market than the weekly close of the market averages by themselves
- how to calculate and chart moving averages for the NYSE and the Amex

Why Moving Averages?

Each day the *Wall Street Journal* publishes a chart of the daily close and the daily range of the Dow for the last three months. Without doubt, it is erratic. It goes up for a few days, then down for a day or two, then up again. Over a period of a few weeks, there might appear to be a downward bias to the data, but as soon as such a bias appears, it is almost surely dissipated by several up days. Looking at the weekly close of the Dow over any short period of time doesn't help either. Let's look at a case history from a four-month period in early 1977 to see how confusing the Dow can be as an indicator of long-term market trends.

CASE HISTORY: Weekly Dow closings in early 1977

WEEK ENDING DATE	DOW CLOSE
7 Jan 1977	983.18
14	972.16
21	962.43
28	957.53
4 Feb	947.89
11	931.52

There is no doubt that over this six-week period, the Dow had been in a steady decline. In other words, the NYSE had been in a *bear market*. Of course, within each week there had been some up days. Most investors on February 11 wished they had sold their total portfolio on January 7. Many also concluded on February 11 that the market was probably going even lower, and decided to bite the bullet and sell with the Dow at 931. Some felt good because they gave up on the market on February 4 and sold out with the Dow at 948.

So what happened the next week? Did the Dow go down some more, as might be expected?

No way!

18 Feb	940.24

Okay, so it went up. Did this mean the market had started a rally after a drop of 5 percent in six weeks? Even the novice investor, anticipating how short-lived this rally might be, would not have been sucked into reinvesting at this point. So what happened to the market over the next four weeks?

25 Feb	933.43
4 Mar	953.46
11 Mar	947.74
18 Mar	961.02

It now seemed that the market was at a bottom on February 11, just when many investors sold. They were now kicking themselves for missing the first thirty points of the new *bull market*, or advance in market averages, which had started. Many reasoned that this new bull market would take the Dow to 1200, so they bought back into the market at 961.

Sorry!

25 March	929.69
1 April	927.36
8 April	918.88

It now appeared they were right back on 11 February; a bear market was indeed in progress, and some advisory services were predicting the Dow would fall to 800 or lower. The smart thing to do seemed to be to sell and take the losses.

Wrong again!

15 April	947.76

The one thing that should be obvious from this case history is that the Dow, or the Amex average also for that matter, of itself can only confuse you. On the other hand, if you had been using a moving average to monitor the weekly market closings throughout the period covered above, you would have been able to conclude that the market was going down and *probably* would continue to go down.

At this point you must learn how to calculate moving averages. Data from the above case will be used so you will see for yourself how much more reliable a moving average is for indicating the true trend of the market.

Calculating Ten-Week Moving Averages

This method works using both the Dow and the Amex average. In terms of calculating moving averages, there is absolutely no difference between the two. The example used here is from the NYSE. You, however, will have to go through this procedure for both the NYSE and the Amex.

Now, in your binder mark one of the dividers "Market Averages." On the first sheet of binder paper following, rule off four columns on the left-hand half of the sheet and head the four columns as follows:

- Date
- Friday Close
- 10-week Total
- 10-week M.A.

Your sheet should look like Figure 3.1.

Now get out your *Wall Street Journal* with last Friday's market data. Record last Friday's date in the tenth space below your column heading, Date. Then record the close of the Dow on the same line. Now you have some research to do, because you must fill in the date and the Friday close for the preceding nine Fridays. You can get this information from back issues of your *Wall Street Journal* or *Barron's* if you've been taking them

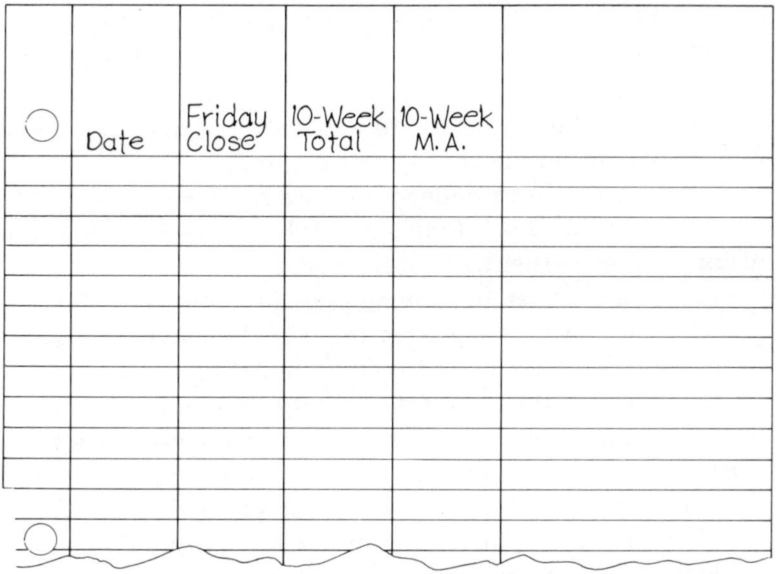

FIGURE 3.1. Your moving averages table

that long, or from copies in your local library, or from your broker.

When you have the first two columns filled for the last ten weeks, you're ready to calculate the ten-week moving average. First, on your calculator total the ten numbers in your Friday Close column. Write this total in the 10-week Total column, on the same line as the most recent entry. Then simply divide this number by 10 and enter the result in the 10-week M.A. column, again on the same line as the most recent entry. That's all there is to calculating a ten-week moving average.

Next Saturday you'll want to add the latest Friday close to your table. To arrive at your new ten-week total, you can simply subtract from your current ten-week total the Friday close at the top of the page, cross through it lightly to keep track that you've done so, and add the latest Friday close. For example, from Table 3.1:

$$\text{Total for March 18} = \text{Total for March 11} + \text{Closing of March 18} - \text{Closing of January 7}$$

Again divide this figure by 10 and enter the new ten-week moving average in the appropriate column.

After you've been under way for a few weeks your table will look like Table 3.1. In this example, figures from the case history related earlier have been used.

Just by looking at the moving average column in Table 3.1, you can tell that the long-term trend of the Dow was downward throughout the period. While the Friday close shows a lot of fluctuation, the ten-week moving average shows a rather smooth, continuous movement in one direction—down. If an investor had observed only the day-to-day changes in the Dow and bought and sold stock accordingly, early 1977 would have been a catastrophe for him or her. On the other hand, the ten-week moving average during this period would have proven a reliable indicator that the economic, financial, political, and other factors that influence the price of stock on the NYSE were pushing prices down and until these factors reversed to mount great pressures to the contrary, the market would probably continue to decrease.

Calculating Fifteen- and Twenty-Week Moving Averages

It is obvious that the ten-week moving average did a remarkably good job of smoothing out the variation in the Dow during the early part of 1977, and in fact it did so throughout the bear market that finally ended on March 31, 1978, with the Dow at 756.36. Likewise, through most bear markets since the Dow was conceived, the ten-week moving average would have to a large extent warned against any premature re-investment in bear markets. It wasn't perfect in all these years, but it was very good.

TABLE 3.1. Calculation of Ten-Week Moving Averages for the NYSE in Early 1977

DATE	FRIDAY CLOSE	10-WK TOTAL	10-WK M.A.
7 Jan 1977	983.18		
14	972.16		
21	962.43		
28	957.53		
4 Feb	947.89		
11	931.52		
18	940.24		
25	933.43		
4 Mar	953.46		
11	947.74	9529.58	953.0
18	961.02	9507.42	950.7
25	929.69	9464.95	946.5
1 Apr	927.36	9429.88	943.0
8	918.88	9391.23	939.1
15	947.76	9391.10	939.1
22	927.07	9386.65	938.7
29	925.80	9372.21	937.2
6 May	936.74	9375.52	937.6
13	928.34	9350.40	935.0
20	930.46	9333.12	933.3

But the ten-week moving average has some shortcomings. For example, for the week ending April 15, 1977, the ten-week moving average was absolutely flat. It had not changed from April 8. Was this the end of the bear market? With hindsight we know it wasn't, but one might have been tempted to start buying stock on April 15. On May 6, an even more positive reading was obtained; the ten-week moving average was up 0.5 points from the previous week's moving average. Of course, we know that this still would have been a terrible time to buy. Watching the ten-week moving average closely is therefore not adequate protection against getting back into the market too soon in a bear market.

There are several ways of overcoming this shortcoming of the ten-week moving average. One is to require that the ten-week moving average rise some number of points, say 2 or 5, before considering the bear market to be over. This criterion would have worked very well to guard against premature decisions on April 15 and on May 6. Another possibility would be to require at least three successive increases in the ten-week moving average before one decides a bear market had ended. Again, this would have worked well on the dates in question. Finally, two additional moving averages, a fifteen- and a twenty-week moving average, can be calculated to guard against premature decisions. These moving averages are even smoother than the ten-week moving average and therefore are more reliable indicators of a reversal in market pressure. They, however, have one defect; the sole use of either one will delay action past the most favorable times to buy or sell. The best strategy is to use all three moving averages simultaneously to make decisions about market directions.

Fifteen- and twenty-week moving averages are calculated in exactly the same way as the ten-week moving average, except that you need fifteen weeks' worth of data to calculate the first fifteen-week moving average, and twenty weeks' worth of data to calculate the first twenty-week moving average. You can tabulate your calculations for all three moving averages on a single sheet of paper. Simply rule off four more columns on the right-hand side of the sheet of binder paper you've already started, and label them with the following headings:

- 15-week Total
- 15-week M.A.
- 20-week Total
- 20-week M.A.

Table 3.2 shows how your table should look when it is fully set up.

During the part of 1977 shown in Table 3.2, only the ten-week moving average rises on May 6; the fifteen-week moving average continues to drop. On May 6, the interpretation of these data must therefore be that the factors that influence the price of stocks on the NYSE are exerting a downward pressure but this pressure is being moderated, maybe only temporarily. This interpretation is confirmed on May 13, when the ten-week moving average again drops. Use of the fifteen- and twenty-week moving averages enables you to interpret more accurately the indications given by the ten-week moving average.

It is important to note here that because the Amex average is much lower than the Dow, due to the lower prices of the stocks listed on the exchange, only ten- and twenty-week moving averages need be calculated for it. Therefore, when you start a sheet in your binder to monitor Amex moving averages, you should set it up with only six columns instead of eight.

Charting Moving Averages

The long-term movement indicated by moving averages can be grasped more quickly and easily if it's plotted on a graph, so take out your graph paper now. Set up charts on two different sheets, one for the NYSE, and one for the Amex.

TABLE 3.2. Calculation of Ten-, Fifteen-, and Twenty-Week Moving Averages for the NYSE in Early 1977

DATE	D.J. CLOSE	10-WK TOTAL	10-WK M.A.	15-WK TOTAL	15-WK M.A.	20-WK TOTAL	20-WK M.A.
7 Jan 1977	983.18						
14	972.16						
21	962.43						
28	957.53						
4 Feb	947.89						
11	931.52						
18	940.24						
25	933.43						
4 Mar	953.46						
11	947.74	9529.58	953.0				
18	961.02	9507.42	950.7				
25	929.69	9464.95	946.5				

1 Apr	927.36	9429.88	943.0				
8	918.88	9391.23	939.1				
15	947.76	9391.10	939.1	14214.29	947.6		
22	927.07	9386.65	938.7	14158.18	943.9		
29	925.80	9372.21	937.2	14111.82	940.8		
6 May	936.74	9375.52	937.6	14086.13	939.1		
13	928.34	9350.40	935.0	14056.94	937.1		
20	930.46	9333.12	933.3	14039.51	936.0	18862.70	943.1

Label the horizontal axis with weekly dates and the vertical axis with market averages at 10-point intervals. For this you'll have to estimate a reasonable range for the high and low points during the period your chart will cover. You can usually track information for about ten months on one sheet of graph paper. In Figure 3.2, the interval between dates has been spread out for clarity. In practice the interval should be about half as large as shown.

When you've got your chart set up, plot the information from your table. For the NYSE, this will be the weekly close of the Dow and the ten-, fifteen-, and twenty-week moving averages. For the Amex, this will be the weekly close of the Amex average and the ten- and twenty-week moving averages. Use a different colored pen or pencil to connect the values you've plotted for each average. Of course, it will take you a number of weeks of accumulating data to start filling your chart out. When it is well underway it should look

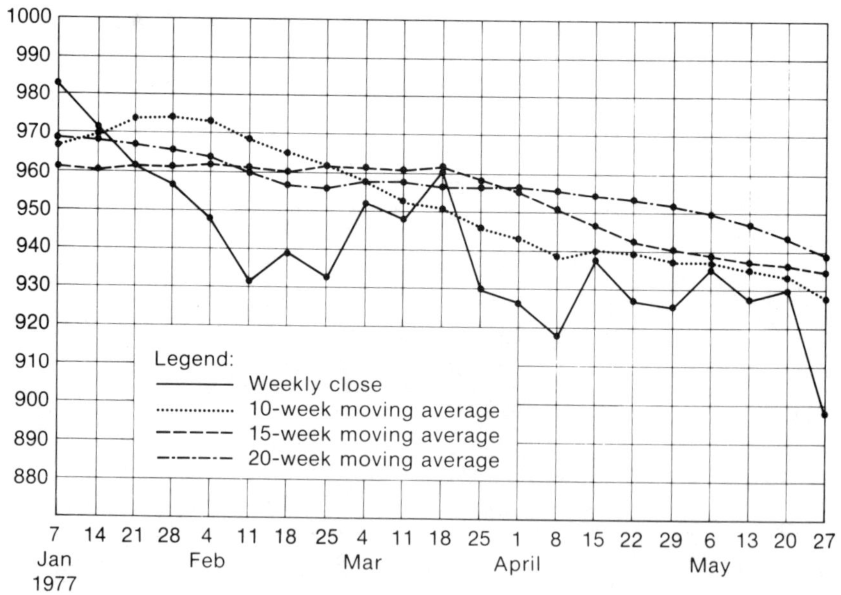

FIGURE 3.2. Charted data for the NYSE in early 1977

something like Figure 3.2. In that figure, all the data for the NYSE for the period in early 1977 that we've been using as an example has been plotted.

Now that you have started collecting your data, you're ready to learn how to interpret it. In the next two chapters you'll learn how to spot bear and bull markets in progress on your chart, and how to establish when they have ended.

Your Action Steps

- Set up your moving averages tables, one with six columns for the Amex and one with eight columns for the NYSE.
- Obtain the Friday close of the two market averages for at least the past ten weeks. If you can obtain data for the past twenty weeks, so much the better: you can start using your data that much faster.
- Begin calculating, every Saturday, the ten-, fifteen-, and twenty-week moving averages for the NYSE and the ten- and twenty-week moving averages for the Amex.
- Set up a chart for the NYSE and one for the Amex and plot information from each table onto the appropriate chart each weekend.

Chapter 4
RECOGNIZING BEAR MARKETS

Now that your data collection is under way, you need to know how to interpret the lines on your moving averages charts. This chapter gives you a simple and clear set of criteria you can use to determine

- when a bear market is in progress
- when a bear market has ended

Bear Markets in Progress

The slopes and relationships of the lines on your moving averages charts tell you a great deal about the nature of the market during the period charted. During a bear market (a market when averages are declining), the lines will be in the following configuration.

Bear market configuration

- All of the moving averages are sloping downward.
- The weekly close of the market average (the Dow or the Amex average) is below all of the moving averages.
- The ten-week moving average is below the fifteen-week moving average (for the Dow) and the twenty-week moving average (for the Dow and the Amex average).
- The fifteen-week moving average is below the twenty-week moving average (for the Dow).

In Figure 4.1 you will note that a bear market was in progress on the NYSE between January 6, 1978, and March 10, 1978. In Figure 4.2 you will note that a bear market was in progress on the Amex between September 19, 1976, and November 19, 1976. You can see that due to the lower average on the Amex at that time, the fluctuations don't look nearly as dramatic as they do on the Dow.

During a bear market, since stock prices in general will be falling, you should avoid buying any stock. Now obviously, in order to obey the first commandment of investing—BUY LOW—you will want to be able to establish as soon as possible after the fact when a bear market has ended. That's the time to do the bulk of your buying. So how do you reliably establish that a bear market has ended? To the tutored eye there are certain unmistakable signs.

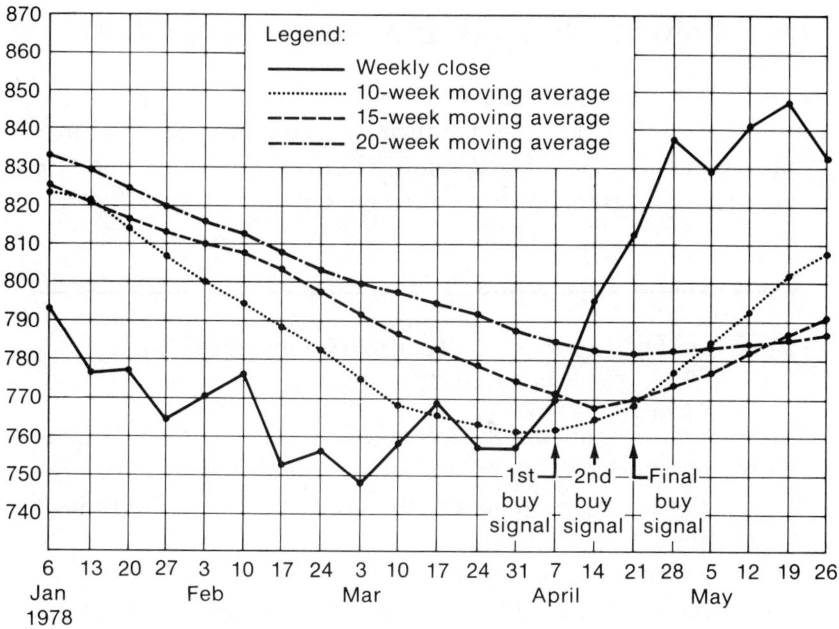

FIGURE 4.1. Bear market in progress and ending on the NYSE, early 1978

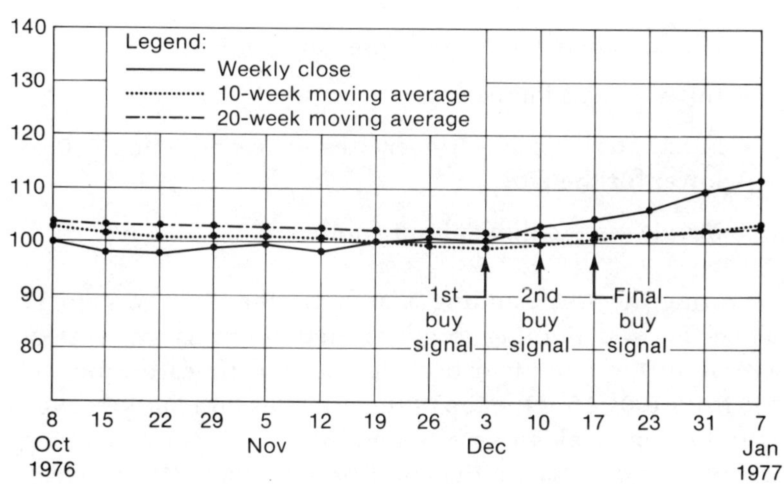

FIGURE 4.2. Bear market in progress and ending on the Amex, late 1976

Establishing That a Bear Market Has Ended

A couple of case histories will be used to give you a feel for how the market behaves when it reaches the end of a bear market and swings upward again. Then a set of criteria will be given to use in interpreting your own current data.

CASE HISTORY: End of a bear market on the NYSE, early 1978

Table 4.1 shows the moving averages data for the NYSE that is charted in Figure 4.1. Refer to both in the description of how the moving averages behaved near and at the true bottom of the market.

In retrospect, it is easy to see that the bottom of the bear market occurred during the week ending Friday, March 3 with the Dow closing at 747.31. But on March 3 there was absolutely no way of knowing that the low point of the bear market had been reached. Likewise, based on the evidence at that time, it would have been foolish to have predicted the start of a bull market.

- All the moving averages were going down.
- Inflation was increasing.
- Stock market advisory services were predicting 600 or lower for the Dow.
- People were talking about another 1929.

During the week ending March 10, the Dow was up 11 points; this was nothing to get excited about as this sort of increase in the Dow had occurred several times during the drop from 1004.65 at the top of the previous bull market. Even the following week's rise of an additional 10 points making the weekly close line on the chart pass through the ten-week moving average line was nothing new; it had occurred several times during this bear market only to be followed by new lows. The retreat of 12 points during the week ending March 24 seemed to confirm that the rise of the previous two weeks was only another pause in the downward spiral.

The First Sign of a Bear Market Ending. The first weak indication that the bear market might be over occurred on April 7, 1978. The Friday close of the Dow was above the ten-week moving average and the ten-week moving average changed direction and increased by 0.5 point. However, this had also happened before; when the Dow was at 840, before the period charted, there was a slight increase for one week in the ten-week moving average. It should be noted at this point that this first very weak sign (which I will call a *buy signal*) appeared five weeks after the true bottom; the Dow had already gone up 22 points from its bear market low. To reiterate one of the premises, you should not expect to buy at the exact bottom of bear markets; this system only helps you buy individual stocks at a low price, and later on sell at a high price.

Three other pieces of information were available to the investor trying to evaluate on April 7 whether the bottom of the bear market had been reached.

- The bear market had been in progress since October 1976 (fifteen months), which is historically a long bear market.
- The ten-week moving average had been flattening out for several weeks.
- Even if it wasn't the bottom of the bear market, the price of some stocks were unbelievably low and at some point in the future would surely sell at a higher price. There were dozens of stocks selling at two times current earnings and in some cases at current earnings. There were stocks paying dividends as high as 25 percent. There were many stocks selling at as low as 20 percent of book value.

TABLE 4.1. Moving Averages for the NYSE in Early 1978 (Averages Circled at Their Low Points)

DATE	FRIDAY CLOSE	10-WK TOTAL	10-WK M.A.	15-WK TOTAL	15-WK M.A.	20-WK TOTAL	20-WK M.A.
6 Jan 1978	793.49	8245.58	824.6	12384.34	825.6	16665.73	833.3
13	775.73	8211.37	821.1	12312.96	820.9	16586.04	829.3
20	776.94	8142.59	814.3	12249.55	816.6	16490.67	824.5
27	764.12	8070.95	807.1	12192.63	812.8	16397.72	819.9
3 Feb	770.50	7997.06	799.7	12154.86	810.3	16311.44	815.6
10	775.99	7949.07	794.9	12108.17	807.2	16248.29	812.4
17	752.69	7886.44	788.6	12050.92	803.4	16153.87	807.7
24	756.24	7827.36	782.7	11961.44	797.4	16069.76	803.5
3 Mar	(747.31)	7744.80	774.5	11872.99	791.5	15995.43	799.8
10	758.58	7671.59	767.2	11787.15	785.8	15945.71	797.3
17	768.71	7646.81	764.7	11731.88	782.1	15891.74	794.6
24	756.70	7627.78	762.8	11673.15	778.2	15838.30	791.9
31	756.36	7607.20	(760.7)	11614.19	774.3	15748.94	787.4

7 Apr	769.58	7612.66	761.3	11553.90	770.3	15682.76	784.1
14	795.13	7637.29	763.7	11518.07	767.9	15633.47	781.7
21	812.80	7674.10	767.4	11537.38	769.2	15622.29	781.1
28	837.32	7758.73	775.9	11598.97	773.3	15644.38	782.2
5 May	829.08	7831.57	783.2	11651.11	776.7	15658.14	782.9
12	840.70	7924.96	792.5	11727.69	781.8	15668.97	783.4
19	846.85	8013.23	801.3	11804.04	786.9	15684.82	784.2
26	831.69	8076.21	807.6	11859.74	790.6	15723.02	786.2

Of course, the above considerations were no guarantee that the bear market was over. There was certainly a risk that the market would go lower and take any stocks that had been purchased at this time with it. On the other hand, however, the potential for profit was also greatest if one began to invest at this first sign. The investor who could afford the risk should certainly have put a percentage of available capital to work at this point. Likewise, those who could afford to take the risk at this time to buy stocks would most likely be those who *went short* (sold stock with an obligation to buy it at a later date) at the start of the bear market. At this time it would certainly have been advisable for such investors to *cover short positions* (buy the stock sold earlier). The percentage of capital to invest at this time was a decision for each investor to make; likewise what to buy was the investor's decision. The subject of what to buy is discussed in detail in Part III. In any case, it was certainly advisable that the amount invested be spread over several different companies.

The Second Buy Signal. The second buy signal appeared on April 14. Look at the chart.

- The weekly close surged above both the fifteen- and twenty-week moving averages.
- The ten-week moving average was up 2 points during the week.
- The fifteen- and twenty-week moving averages appeared to be flattening out.
- Calculation of the potential fifteen- and twenty-week moving averages, presuming even a modest increase in the Dow over the next few weeks, indicated that they *could* change direction shortly.
- The Dow was at a new high for the year.
- Even if the Dow retreated 15 points in the next week, the ten-week moving average would still be up next week.

- Even if the Dow retreated 15 points during the next week, the fifteen-week moving average would be flat, not down.

Based on all of the above, the risks for investors seemed to be lower than they had been on April 7. The potential for profit was almost as good as it was on April 2 since many stocks meeting our buying criterion (described in Chapter 8) had not increased in price. Even the most conservative investor should have utilized a portion of capital at this point to purchase a few best buys. The investor who could afford the risk was already partially invested at this point and certainly should have added to the amount invested at this time.

The Third Buy Signal. On April 21, the third buy signal appeared. The death of the bear market was apparent.

- The weekly close of the Dow was above all the moving averages.
- The ten-week moving average was accelerating upward.
- The fifteen-week moving average had turned upward.
- The twenty-week moving average was almost flat.
- Unless there were a horrible drop in the Dow in the next week, the ten-week moving average would pass through and exceed the fifteen-week moving average.
- The Dow was at a new high for the year.
- Presuming even a modest increase in the Dow over the next few weeks, the ten-week moving average would pass through and exceed the twenty-week moving average.
- Even in the event of a decrease of 25 points in the Dow in the next week, the fifteen-week moving average would still be up.

All but the most timid should have committed the remainder of their capital at this time. Many great buys were still available. The aggressive investor who started buying the week following the first signal of April 7 might even have had a few stocks that had gone too far too fast. These should have been sold and some other stocks should have been bought. Certainly, the aggressive investor should have been fully invested at this time and possibly considering some margin purchases.

CASE HISTORY: *End of a bear market on the Amex, late 1976*

Table 4.2 shows the moving averages data for the Amex that is charted in Figure 4.2. Refer to both during the description of the succession of buy signals that appeared as the bear market reached bottom and swung upward.

The First Buy Signal. The typical bear market configuration existed until November 19. On November 26, the Friday close of the Amex average was above the ten-week moving average but the ten-week moving average was still going down. On December 3, the ten-week moving average was flat and it could be calculated that a small increase in the next week in the Amex average would cause the ten-week average to go up. This was the time to start buying on the Amex. In the case of the NYSE, the ten-week moving average must turn up before a buy signal is indicated.

The Second Buy Signal. The second strong buy signal appeared on December 10.

- The Friday close of the Amex average was substantially above both the ten- and twenty-week moving averages.
- The ten-week moving average was going up.

TABLE 4.2 Moving Averages for the Amex in Late 1976 (Averages Circled at Their Low Points)

DATE	FRIDAY CLOSE	10-WK TOTAL	10-WK M.A.	20-WK TOTAL	20-WK M.A.
8 Oct 1976	99.96	1024.64	102.5	2068.80	103.4
15	98.21	1019.44	101.9	2063.85	103.2
22	(97.88)	1013.52	101.4	2059.53	103.0
29	98.88	1010.61	101.1	2055.64	102.8
5 Nov	99.72	1008.90	100.9	2050.47	102.5
12	98.55	1004.85	100.5	2043.96	102.2
19	100.04	1001.86	100.2	2038.83	101.9
26	100.52	999.00	99.9	2032.28	101.6
3 Dec.	100.15	995.47	(99.5)	2026.91	101.4
10	103.20	997.11	99.7	2025.46	(101.3)
17	104.07	1001.22	100.1	2025.86	101.3
23	105.91	1008.92	100.9	2029.36	101.5
31	109.84	1020.88	101.7	2034.40	101.7
7 Jan 1977	110.94	1032.94	102.9	2043.55	102.2

- It could be calculated that even a modest increase in the Amex average over the next few weeks would turn the twenty-week average up.

The Final Buy Signal. The final buy signal appeared on December 17.

- The Friday close of the Amex average was above both of the moving averages.

- The ten-week moving average was moving up.
- The twenty-week moving average was flat.
- It could be calculated that only a small increase in the Amex average over the next few weeks would cause the ten-week average to exceed the twenty-week moving average.
- It could be calculated that a very small increase in the Amex average would cause the twenty-week average to turn up.

The typical bull market configuration appeared on January 7, 1977.

As you can see from these case histories, the various moving averages are progressively less sensitive to fluctuations in the Friday close of the market average. The first sign that a bear market has ended appears in the Friday close, but at the time it is impossible to tell whether this is really a decisive upturn or merely signals the start of a short-lived rally. The market could certainly swing down again.

When the Friday close of the market average moves above the ten-week moving average and the ten-week moving average turns up, this is a fairly strong sign that the factors pushing the average up are gaining momentum and will continue upward for some time. At this point, called the first buy signal, even if you are a conservative investor you should invest a portion of your capital. Notice you haven't been told what to invest in yet; that is taken up later in the book. Right now it's more important for you to get a feel for the market.

By the time the slowest-moving and least sensitive indicator, the twenty-week moving average, reaches bottom and shows the first slight increase, the death of the bear market is certain. Of course, by this time most other investors know this, too, so if you buy now you have less competitive edge. Lots of certainty, but less potential for profit. You can get a slight edge by forecasting what the fifteen- and twenty-week moving averages would be if the market average increased by a certain reasonably likely number of points. The method for doing this is quick and easy.

Forecasting Moving Averages

In the first case above, under the second buy signal, it says "Calculation of the potential fifteen- and twenty-week moving averages, presuming even a modest increase in the Dow over the next few weeks, indicated that they *could* change direction shortly." Potential moving averages are calculated when the ten-week moving average flattens out. Presume an increase of 10 to 15 points in the Dow each week for three weeks. Write these potential figures for the Dow into the moving averages tables using a pencil, and then calculate what the corresponding ten-, fifteen-, and twenty-week moving averages would be. Of course these data and potential moving averages are erased after the actual Dow closings are obtained and the real ten-, fifteen-, and twenty-week moving averages are calculated.

Marking Buy Signals on Your Charts

The following is a summary of the criteria discussed for determining when to start buying as the market appears to be changing directions, from a downward trend to an upward one.

Mark the first buy signal on your chart when . . .

- the Friday close is above the ten-week moving average, *and*

- the ten-week moving average shows a slight increase or is flat but you can calculate that a moderate increase in the market average in the next week would cause the ten-week moving average to go up.

Mark the second buy signal on your chart when . . .

- the Friday close is above the ten-week moving average, *and*
- the ten-week moving average is moving upward, *and*
- the fifteen- and twenty-week moving averages appear to be flattening out, *and*
- you can calculate that a moderate increase in the market average will cause the fifteen- and twenty-week moving averages to swing upward.

Mark the final buy signal on your chart when . . .

- the Friday close of the market average is above all the moving averages, *and*
- the ten-week moving average maintains its upward direction, *and*
- the fifteen-week moving average starts to swing upward, *and*
- the twenty-week moving average flattens out, *and*
- you can calculate that a moderate increase in the market average will cause the ten-week moving average to move above the fifteen-week moving average.

Your Action Steps

- Study your moving averages charts for the NYSE and the Amex.
- Use the criteria in this chapter to determine if either shows a bear market configuration.
- If so, monitor the progress of the moving averages closely and mark buy signals when you have identified them according to the criteria in this chapter.

Chapter 5
IDENTIFYING BULL MARKETS

Just as there is a typical bear market configuration and certain recognizable signs when a bear market has ended, there is a typical bull market configuration and certain recognizable signs when a bull market has ended. This chapter gives you a simple and clear set of criteria to determine

- when a bull market is in progress
- when a bull market has ended

Bull Markets in Progress

It stands to reason that the configuration of a bull market (a market when averages are advancing) in progress would be the inverse of the configuration of a bear market in progress. This is indeed the case.

Bull Market Configuration

- All of the moving averages are sloping upward.
- The weekly close of the market average (the Dow or the Amex average) is above all of the moving averages.
- The ten-week moving average is above the fifteen-week moving average (for the Dow) and the twenty-week moving average (for the Dow and the Amex average).
- The fifteen-week moving average is above the twenty-week moving average (for the Dow).

In Figure 5.1 you will note that a bull market was in progress on the NYSE between December 1, 1972, and January 19, 1973. In Figure 5.2 you will note that a bull market was in progress on the Amex between June 6, 1975, and July 18, 1975. Again, since the Amex average is lower than the Dow, its fluctuations don't look nearly as dramatic.

During a bull market, since stock prices in general will be rising, the best position for you to be in is to have invested your capital heavily at the beginning of the bull market and to hold on to your stock until the top of the bull market, when you begin selling. This is the ideal, but of course we know that the reality will fall short of this. In reality, you can continue buying throughout the bull market, when you find a stock that is underpriced, and selling stocks when they reach a fair price or above. We will discuss this in further detail in Chapter 8 when we talk about the stocks. Also in reality, you will not be able to identify that a bull market has reached its peak until after the fact. Still, by paying close attention to certain unmistakable signals, you can hope to sell fairly high before the

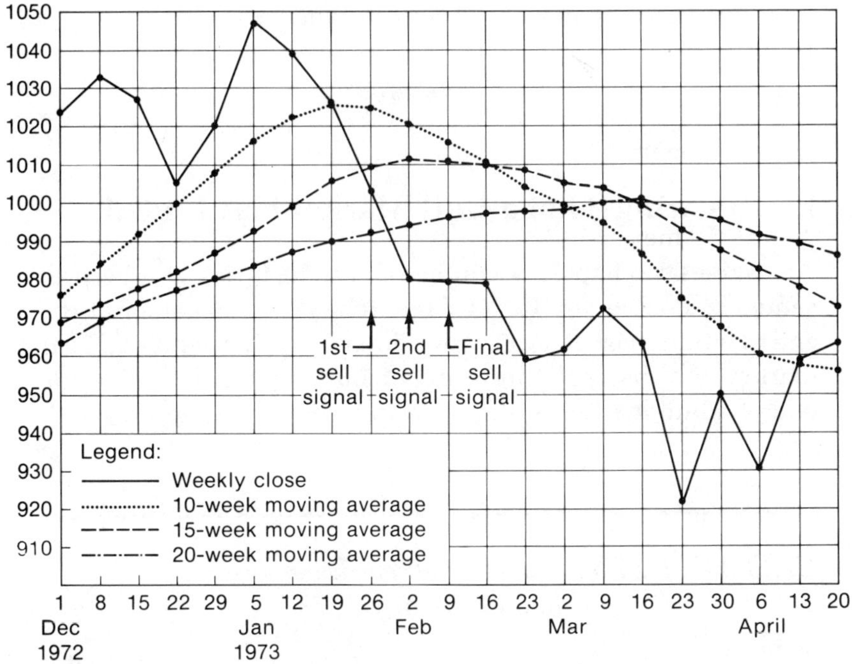

FIGURE 5.1. *Bull market in progress and ending on the NYSE, late 1972–early 1973*

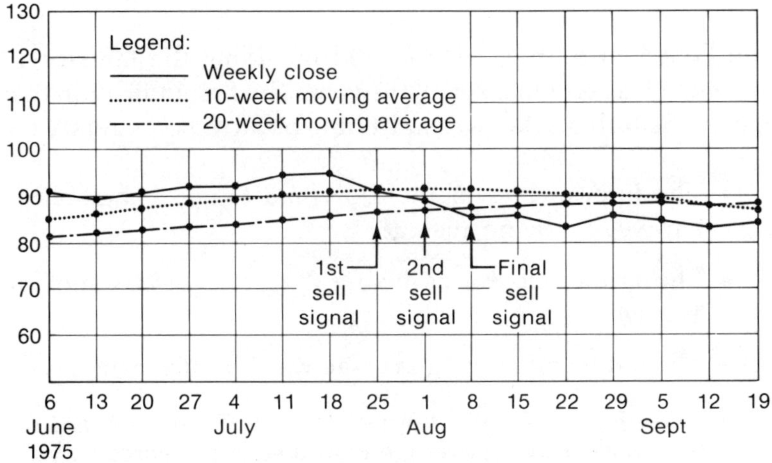

FIGURE 5.2. *Bull market in progress and ending on the Amex, mid-1975*

new bear market is well underway, and can hope to turn a profit.

Establishing That a Bull Market Has Ended

As in the last chapter, a couple of case histories will be presented to enable you to get a feel for market behavior at the end of a bull market as it swings downward. The end of a bear market was discussed in terms of buy signals. Likewise the end of a bull market is discussed in terms of *sell signals*.

CASE HISTORY: End of a bull market on the NYSE, late 1972–early 1973

Table 5.1 shows the moving averages data for the NYSE that is charted in Figure 5.1. Refer to both as the behavior of the moving averages is described near and at the true top of the market.

The First Sell Signal. Up to and including the January 19 closing, it was bull market all the way. The first indication that maybe the bull market was in trouble occurred on January 26.

- The Friday close of the Dow had fallen to below the ten-week moving average.
- The Friday close was below the fifteen-week moving average.
- The ten-week moving average was not increasing.
- Even if the Dow did not go down in the next week, the ten-week moving average would start to decrease.

- The bull market was aged. It had started in July of 1970 and was two-and-a-half years old. It was time for it to die or have a severe setback.

At this point, conservative investors should have sold at least 20 percent of their portfolios and put the cash into treasury bills or other cash equivalents. The aggressive investor who could afford the risk should likewise have sold a portion of the portfolio but the proceeds should have been used to go short.

The Second Sell Signal. The second sell signal appeared on February 2.

- The Dow continued to drop.
- The Dow was below all three moving averages.
- The ten-week moving average had turned down.
- The fifteen-week moving average was flattening out.
- It could be calculated that even if the Dow did not decrease in the next week, the fifteen-week moving average would go down.

The prudent investor should have made plans at this point to sell all the stock in his or her portfolio.

The Final Sell Signal. By February 9, the death of the bull market was almost a certainty.

- The ten-week moving average was decreasing at a rate of 5 points per week.
- The fifteen-week moving average was decreasing at a rate of 1 point per week. It could be calculated that the rate of decrease would become larger with any reasonable projection for the Dow over the next few weeks.

TABLE 5.1. *Moving Averages for the NYSE in Early 1973 (Averages Circled at Their High Points)*

DATE	FRIDAY CLOSE	10-WK TOTAL	10-WK M.A.	15-WK TOTAL	15-WK M.A.	20-WK TOTAL	20-WK M.A.
1 Dec 1972	1023.93	9752.12	975.2	14533.19	968.9	19263.89	963.2
8	1033.19	9832.04	983.2	14596.33	973.1	19376.63	968.8
15	1027.44	9914.12	991.4	14662.53	977.5	19477.93	973.9
22	1004.21	9987.87	998.8	14719.42	981.3	19530.42	976.5
29	1020.02	10065.08	1006.5	14796.63	986.4	19586.26	979.3
5 Jan 1973	1047.49	10166.15	1016.6	14890.85	992.7	19667.92	983.4
12	1039.36	10221.39	1022.1	14984.85	999.0	19747.92	987.4
19	1026.19	10252.32	1025.2	15080.58	1005.4	19804.06	990.2
26	1003.54	10250.29	1025.0	15141.31	1009.4	19846.36	992.3
2 Feb	980.81	10206.18	1020.6	15175.70	1011.7	19879.85	994.0
9	979.46	10161.71	1016.2	15171.04	1011.4	19917.50	995.9
16	979.23	10107.75	1010.8	15155.01	1010.3	19943.46	997.2
23	959.89	10040.20	1004.0	15119.64	1008.0	19957.99	997.9

2 Mar	961.32	9997.31	999.7	15075.39	1005.0	19978.85	998.9
9	972.23	9949.50	995.0	15058.31	1003.9	19998.27	999.9
16	962.97	9865.00	986.5	14997.35	999.8	20014.82	1000.7
23	922.71	9748.35	974.8	14885.87	992.5	19953.41	997.7
30	951.08	9673.24	967.3	14810.50	987.4	19909.23	995.5
6 Apr	931.07	9600.77	960.1	14737.37	982.5	19834.73	991.7
13	959.36	9579.32	957.9	14676.71	978.4	19785.50	989.3
20	963.35	9563.21	956.3	14592.58	972.8	19724.92	986.2

- The twenty-week moving average was flattening out.
- The Friday closing of the Dow was below all the moving averages.
- It could be calculated that even if the Dow went up a little during the next few weeks, the ten-week moving average would drop to below the twenty-week moving average.

At this point the conservative investor should have sold everything. Of course, as it turned out this was good advice for every investor. As in the case of bear markets, there was no way of knowing on January 5 that the top of the bull market had been reached. By February 9, the date of the final sell signal, the market had decreased by 6.4 percent and presumably investors had lost the same percentage on the stocks that were still in their portfolios. Still, February 9 wasn't a bad time to sell, with the Dow at about 980, considering that it finally bottomed at 577.60 in December 1974. Figure 5.1 shows the typical bear market configuration after March 23. While waiting for the next bull market to start, the conservative investor should have invested in treasury bills or certificates of deposit. The aggressive investor should have been in a 100 percent short position.

CASE HISTORY: End of a bull market on the Amex, mid-1975

Table 5.2 shows the moving averages data for the Amex that is charted in Figure 5.2. Refer to both during the following description of the succession of sell signals that appeared as the bull market reached the top and swung downward.

The First Sell Signal. The first indication that the bull market was topping out occurred July 25 when the weekly close of

TABLE 5.2. Moving Averages for the Amex in Mid-1975 (Averages Circled at Their High Points)

DATE	FRIDAY CLOSE	10-WK TOTAL	10-WK M.A.	20-WK TOTAL	20-WK M.A.
6 Jun 1975	90.69	854.35	85.4	1624.54	81.2
13	89.43	864.77	86.5	1642.92	82.2
20	91.08	874.61	87.5	1659.80	83.0
27	93.00	884.66	88.5	1677.72	83.9
4 Jul	92.60	893.85	89.4	1693.53	84.7
11	95.27	904.94	90.5	1711.07	85.6
18	(95.67)	913.22	91.3	1729.47	86.5
25	91.14	917.25	91.7	1742.95	87.2
1 Aug	89.23	918.75	(91.9)	1752.18	87.6
8	85.86	915.98	91.6	1757.57	87.9
15	86.16	911.40	91.1	1763.72	88.2
22	83.58	905.55	90.6	1768.29	(88.4)
29	86.64	901.11	90.1	1773.48	88.7
5 Sep	85.45	893.56	89.4	1774.75	88.7
12	88.48	884.44	88.4	1773.32	88.7
19	84.56	873.33	87.3	1770.49	88.5

the Amex average dropped below the ten-week moving average. The rate of increase of the ten-week moving average was also decreasing. There was a good possibility that this could have been a false signal; however, it was a good time to clean up one's portfolio by selling a portion of those stocks that had substantially increased in price.

The Second Sell Signal. On August 1, the prospects for Amex stocks showed further deterioration.

- The weekly close was well below the ten-week moving average.
- The ten-week moving average was almost flat.
- It could be calculated that even if the Amex average did not go down in the next week, the ten-week moving average would go down.

At this point, prudent investors should have further reduced their portfolios.

The Final Sell Signal. The final sell signal appeared on August 8.

- The weekly close of the Amex average had dropped below both the ten- and twenty-week moving averages.
- The ten-week moving average had turned down.
- The twenty-week moving average was flattening.
- It could be calculated that a small decrease in the Amex average over the next few weeks would cause the twenty-week moving average to turn down.

At this point the prudent investor should have sold some more stocks. Based on the remainder of the chart and the performance of the Amex over the next two years, all this selling proved to have been unnecessary. But on the dates in question, one had no way of knowing that the slide in the Amex would not duplicate the catastrophe of 1973–74 when it dropped 60 percent. Remember, the system described here is intended to produce profits during bull markets and to protect these profits in bear markets or possible bear markets. The death of the bull continued to be confirmed through August. The typical bear market configuration appeared on September 19; the Friday close of the Amex average was below the ten-week moving average which was below the twenty-week moving average and both of the moving averages were going down.

It should be noted here that Figure 5.2 showed the performance of the Amex in 1975 when the index was less than 100 and a 10-point swing was important. By mid-1978, the chart of the Amex average looked dramatically different because the index was at a much higher level, as shown in Figure 5.3. By late 1979, the chart of the Amex average had changed again, with the index price level as shown in Figure 5.4.

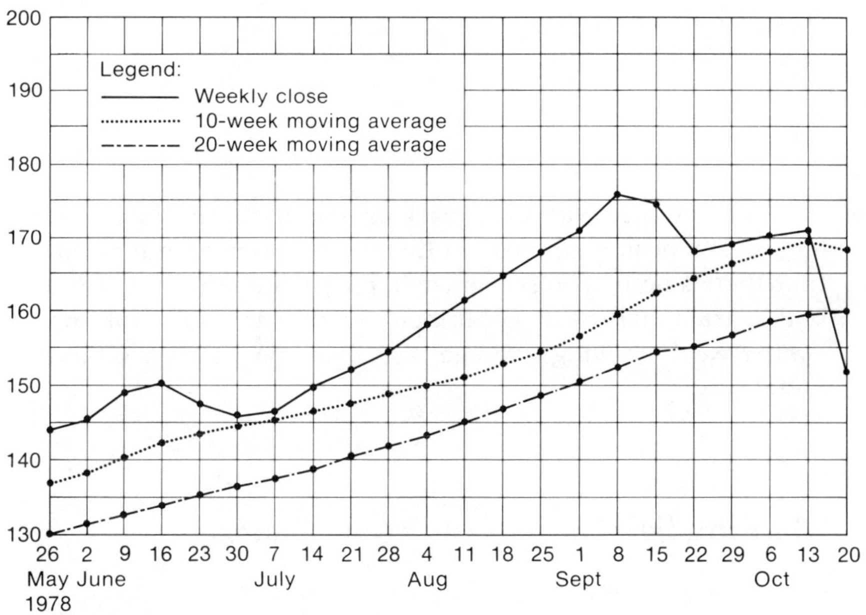

FIGURE 5.3. Amex averages in mid-1978

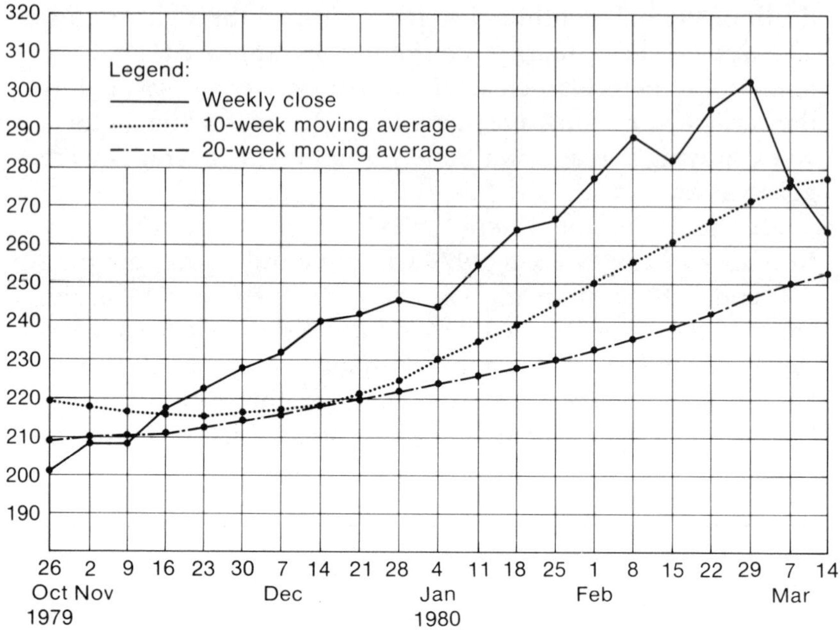

FIGURE 5.4. Amex averages in late 1979–early 1980

As is the case with bear markets, the first sign that a bull market has peaked appears in the market average, but at the time there's no way to recognize it. By the time the end of the bull market has been confirmed by the downturn of the twenty-week moving average, the bear market has gotten under way.

Marking Sell Signals on Your Charts

So in summary, the following are the criteria for determining when to start selling as the market appears to be changing direction, from an upward trend to a downward one.

Mark the first sell signal on your chart when . . .

- the Friday close is below the ten-week moving average, *and*
- the ten-week moving average shows a slight decrease or is flat but you can calculate that a moderate decrease in the market average in the next week would cause the ten-week moving average to go down.

Mark the second sell signal on your chart when . . .

- the Friday close of the market average is below the ten-week moving average, *and*
- the ten-week moving average is moving downward, *and*
- the fifteen- and twenty-week moving averages appear to be flattening out, *and*
- you can calculate that a moderate decrease in the market average will cause the fifteen- and twenty-week moving averages to swing downward.

Mark the final sell signal on your chart when . . .

- the Friday close of the market average is below the moving averages, *and*
- the ten-week moving average maintains its downward direction, *and*
- the fifteen-week moving average starts to swing downward, *and*
- the twenty-week moving average flattens out, *and*
- you can calculate that a moderate decrease in the

market average will cause the ten-week moving average to drop below the fifteen-week moving average.

Your Action Steps

- Study your moving averages charts for the NYSE and the Amex.
- Use the criteria in this chapter to determine if either shows a bull market configuration.
- If so, monitor the progress of the moving averages closely and mark sell signals when you have identified them according to the criteria in this chapter.

Chapter 6

ANTICIPATING MASSACRES

So far we have established that by watching moving averages and the Friday close of the Dow and the Amex average, you can identify bull and bear markets in progress and can recognize their endings after the fact. Sometimes the market drops too fast for moving averages to give you useful information, as was the case in October 1978 and 1979. This chapter discusses a couple of tools you can use to increase your sensitivity to large short-term drops in the market:

- trend lines and channels
- the daily pulse of the market

What Is a Massacre?

A massacre is a short-term plunge in the market. The word *massacre* was coined by the press specifically to describe the October 1978 disaster on the NYSE and Amex. In the midst of a bull market that had started on March 3 (we identified the start of this bull market in one of our case histories in Chapter 4), the market reached a peak on October 13 and then plunged nearly 90 points in the space of two short weeks. From there it began another slow trend upward until October 5, 1979, when it took another plunge of 70 points in the space of two weeks.

Is there any way to anticipate such massacres when the average drops by as much as 70 or 80 points over a period of a few weeks in the midst of a longer-term trend upward? Yes. There are certain signals you can pick up if you are watching the daily pulse of the market.

Using Trend Lines and Channels

A *trend line* is a line that can be drawn connecting two or more peaks or valleys on the charts of the daily or weekly market average close, or of individual stock prices. The space between upper and lower trend lines that are approximately parallel is called a *channel*. See Figure 6.1 for an example. For the most part, though the market will trend over the long term in the direction of the trend lines, the marked average will fluctuate pretty neatly within the channel. When the market average approaches the top or bottom of the channel, it's a sign that the market is in for some kind of readjustment, and that you should be on the alert. When the market average leaves the channel it is a sign that a market reversal is under way.

To spot possible trend lines, look at peaks and valleys formed by the Friday close line on your moving averages chart for each exchange. Where any two peaks or valleys line up, you can draw a tentative line. Look for a possible upper and

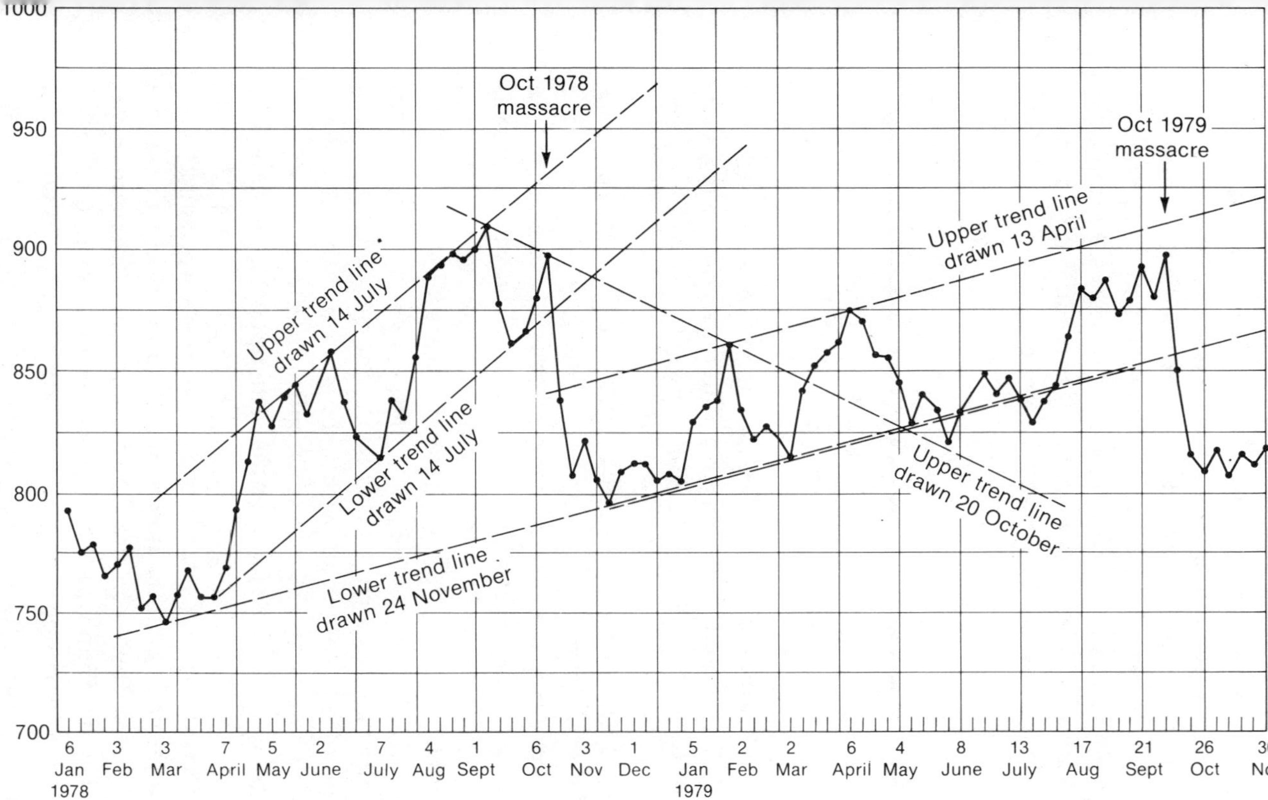

FIGURE 6.1. *Trend lines and channels based on Friday close of the Dow, Jan. 1978–Nov. 1979*

lower line. They don't have to be exactly parallel to each other, but they may be. The following case history discusses how and when the trend lines in Figure 6.1 were drawn. Note this is the same chart that was used to record the Friday close and moving averages of the Dow. However, the moving averages have been removed and the time scale compressed for clarity and to cover a greater time span. After reading it you should have a better feel for how to do it yourself.

CASE HISTORY: Trend lines and channels on the NYSE, 1978 and 1979

The Bull Market of 1978. The bull market of 1978 started on March 3. This period was described in terms of moving averages in Chapter 4. These moving averages would have been the only indicators available to the investor until July 14. During the first part of this bull market, the Dow rose to about 860 before correcting to about 812 on July 7. During the following week, the Dow rose and closed out the week at 840. But on July 7, the investor had no idea which way the Dow was going to go (except of course, that the moving averages were in a bull market configuration). After the next week was over, the investor could see that the July 7 market close was the bottom of a valley and as such provided a point on a lower trend line. This point was connected with a straight line to the March 31 low point to extablish a lower trend line; this line was then extrapolated for several months. An upper trend line was drawn through the April, May, and June peaks parallel to the lower trend line. This upper trend line was surprisingly close to a tentative upper line drawn on June 16 connecting the three upper peaks. Between these two trend lines, a channel was established within which one expected the Dow to meander.

The Dow cooperated perfectly during July, August, and September, and the first two weeks in October. On October 13, the Dow was in its channel and the moving averages were all trending up. The investor who was watching the daily close would have been alert when the average left its established channel at the start of the massacre, about October 16. By the week ending October 20, the market had all the appearances of the start of a bear market. An investor who had been alert to the warning given by the trend lines would have sold out before the massacre reached bottom.

A New Upper Trend Line. On October 20, 1978, there was no question that the old trend lines had been broken. A new upper trend line was drawn connecting the peak of September 8 and the peak of October 13. This new upper trend line was pointing down in a typical bear market mode; the moving averages, likewise, had all turned down. At this point in time no lower trend line could be drawn and therefore, at this time, there was no channel. On November 3, a tentative lower trend line was drawn between the low of October 27 and the low of March 3. This trend line was pointing up. This tentative lower trend line, however, was violated on November 17 and a new tentative line was drawn on November 24. This new lower limit was confirmed on January 5, 1979; the ten-week moving average was also positive at this time but the other moving averages were still negative.

On February 2, 1979, the tentative downward-trending upper trend line that was drawn October 20, 1978, was confirmed; the January 26 peak was exactly on the downward-sloping upper trend line and the Dow had retreated from this upper trend line. The upward-sloping lower trend line was again confirmed on March 9. The Dow therefore had established over five months an upper trend line sloping down and a lower trend line sloping up and a channel converging at about 825 for the week ending May 4. A bull market channel was established on April 13; the upper trend line connected the peaks of January 26 and April 6. The Dow stayed within this channel until October 5. The following two weeks constituted the October 1979 massacre. The lower trend line drawn on November 24, 1978 was decisively violated and the search for a new trend line was started.

You can see that trend lines and channels can be useful tools. They work for both the Amex average and the Dow; they can warn against massacres and also indicate when to buy and sell during an established bull market. As the Dow approaches the top of an established bull market channel, you are advised to sell at least 20 percent of your portfolio even though the moving averages are in a bull market configuration. Likewise, when the market average has hit the bottom of an established bull market channel and has turned upward, you are advised to buy some stocks. In Chapter 8 you'll see how individual stock prices also tend to fluctuate in channels, and how you can make buying and selling decisions by juxtaposing the data you have about market average channels and individual stock price channels.

Now we will turn to the daily pulse of the market, a chart you must keep if you want to stay closely tuned in to the market.

The Daily Pulse of the Market

Keeping a chart for each exchange that shows the daily close of the market average, volume traded, and number of issues that advanced and declined will take you only a few minutes each night and will provide you with valuable information. You can draw trend lines on it, and compare it with the moving averages and long-term trend line charts, to get a good feel for daily market behavior. The following shows how to chart this data. Then a couple of case histories show you how to use it, and guidelines are given for interpreting the data.

Setting Up Your Chart. You will need to obtain from your broker or *Wall Street Journal* the following daily data:

- close of the Dow and the Amex average
- total volume of stocks traded on each exchange
- number of issues that advanced on each exchange
- number of issues that declined on each exchange

Now look at Figure 6.2. Friday dates are marked on the horizontal axis. The bottom portion of the vertical axis is marked to show volume in millions. The daily volume is plotted as a bar. The middle portion of the vertical axis is marked to show number of issues advancing/declining. Each evening the number of advancing issues is plotted with a black dot, and the number of declining issues is plotted with a red dot. Then each dot is connected with the dot of the same color from the day before. If the number of advancing issues exceeds the number of declining issues the day before, and the number of declining issues exceeds the number of advancing issues the day before, the lines will cross. Color in the space that is defined in this way with the color of the dots that are on top. Last, the top portion of the vertical axis is marked to show the market closing average, and the data is plotted as on the other market average charts. Trend lines are drawn too, as you can see.

Now go ahead and set these two new charts up, one for each exchange. Then follow Figure 6.2 (which covers the same period on the NYSE that was described in the discussion of moving averages in Chapter 4) as you read the following case history.

CASE HISTORY: The daily pulse of the NYSE, January–April 1978

On January 1, 1978, the Dow was on its way down to the lower trend line. It then meandered sideways near the lower trend

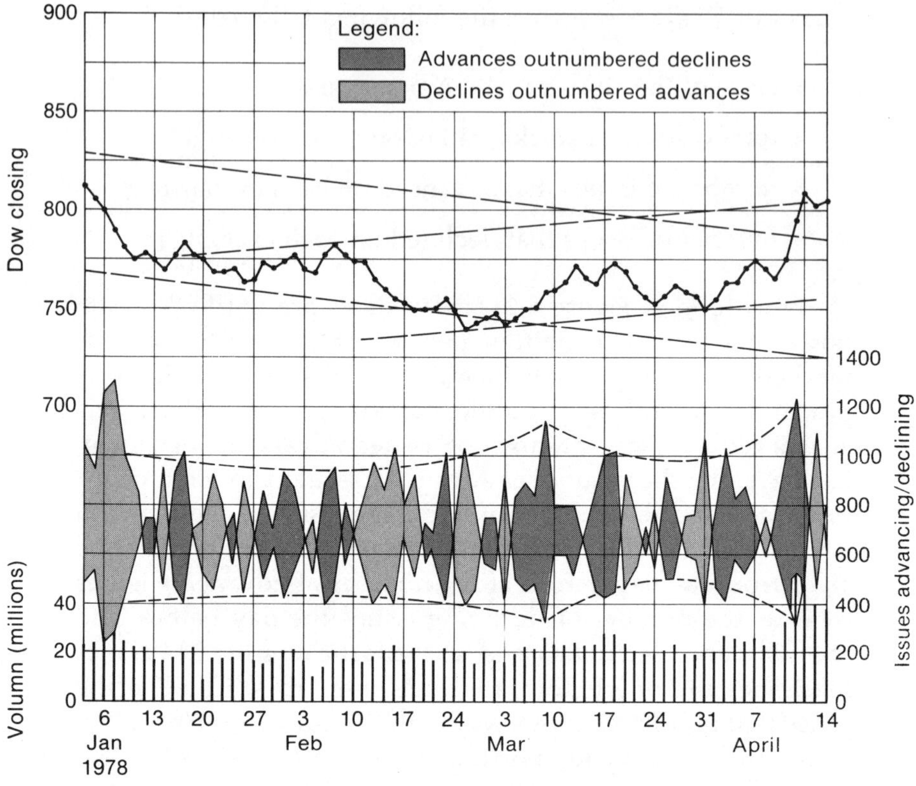

FIGURE 6.2. The daily pulse of the NYSE, Jan.–Apr. 1978

line for about four weeks before again dropping to touch the line. A rally started on March 3 and took the Dow to 772 on March 12. The action of the Dow during the latter part of March and early April while still in a bear channel was definitely flattening out. On April 4, an investor could draw the first, very tentative lower bull market trend line. A tentative upper bull market trend line could be drawn parallel to this line through the February 6 peak. Confirmation of the bull market came on April 14 when the Dow passed above the upper limit of the old bear market channel. The tentative bull market channel was justified at this time for a variety of reasons, not the least of which was that the bear market had been in progress for a long time and was due to end. We were expecting a bull market to start and should have been searching for the first signs.

If a large volume of stock is traded on an up day on the Dow, this indicates upward pressure. On the other hand, if the market is up on a slow day of trading, it has little meaning regarding the pressure on the market. The upturn during the first half of March by the Dow was matched with higher volume, whereas the drop in the Dow in February was during low volume. Likewise, the correction in the latter part of March was also during low volume. The volume of 28 million shares on April 5 with the Dow up was more than enough evidence to start reinvesting. Today, of course, 28 million shares would be a quiet day.

A particularly harsh period in a bear market is marked by a severe decrease in the Dow with high volume and a large number of declining issues and few advancing issues. The first week and a half of January 1978 was such a period. The remainder of January and all of February, however, showed only mild peaks on the occasions of greater declines than advances as well as the occasions of greater advances than declines. The advance of the Dow during the first two weeks of March was accompanied by high volume as noted earlier, which was encouraging, but even more encouraging was the fact that for two weeks there were more advances than declines and that on April 9, the peak for the number of advancing issues was substantially higher than any advancing-issue peak of the last six months. Then the correction of April 22, 23, and 24 created only a small peak on declining volume, indicating that many stocks were resisting any downward movement.

Finally, it will be noted that if one connects the tops of the advancing-issue peaks with a dotted line and does the same thing with the advancing-issue valleys, definite cycles of swells and recessions will be defined by the lines. On April 5 and 6 it appeared that the trend of advances over declines was increasing and that sometime in the near future a real rally with 1100 to 1300 advances might occur. With this evidence as well as the evidence provided by the weekly moving average chart, an investor could have anticipated the market bottom. Another vital piece of evidence was available on April 5, 1978. The NYSE had been in a bear market since September of 1976 (one and a half years) which is traditionally a long bear market. The market seemed ready at least for a substantial rally, and at best for a big bull market.

A few more words should be said about the channels that are drawn on this working chart. One will be amazed at how long the Dow will move within such a channel established early in either a bull or bear market. Don't hesitate, however, to revise the width or slope of the channel as more data becomes available. In one case, the Dow stayed within a 50-point upward channel from December 1976 till July 1977. The channel then became slightly steeper and 60 points wide until April 1978.

After an up-channel has been established in a bull market, this information is used for the proper timing of the sale of stocks that have reached a high price and for the purchase of stocks to replace those sold. Wait until the Dow is close to the bottom of the channel to buy and wait until the Dow is close to the top of the channel to sell.

After a down-channel has been established in a bear market, use this information to eliminate any stocks that you might have been caught holding. For example, after the October 1978 massacre most investors would have been caught holding more stock than desirable. By January 29, however, a potential channel had been established and if one didn't believe a new bull market was imminent, January 29, 1979, was an excellent opportunity to unload.

CASE HISTORY: *The daily pulse of the NYSE, July–November 1978*

Figure 6.3 is an example of the information that is given by these charts during a bull market and at the top of a bull market. This data for the period July–November 1978 covers the massacre of October 1978. The Dow is plotted at the top. It was a typical bull market; the Dow was generally moving up in a channel 70 points wide. Of course, the ten-, fifteen-, and twenty-week moving averages were also going up in typical bull market configuration. The summer rally in July was quite pronounced. Volume was high, reaching 60 million shares on August 2. Advance/decline figures were bullish. The remainder of the summer and into the fall was quite normal. Even the drop in the Dow in the middle of September still stayed within the long-term channel. The volume, however, stayed relatively high—36 to 41 million shares. This was bearish.

The true warning was sounded during the three weeks of advances by the Dow in late September and early October; volume dropped during the advance to an average of about 24 million shares per day. Even the most aggressive investor and the newest novice in the market should have sold everything on the basis of this information before the October massacre. There was also another piece of evidence available in the advance/decline data; the Dow was going up, but the advancing issues were only slightly higher than the declining issues during this period.

One other piece of information was available from the chart. If a smooth line were drawn connecting the advancing-issue peaks of the advance/decline data and a second line were drawn between the declining-issue peaks of the advance/decline data, one obtained some swooping lines that were quite periodic. Around the middle of September, the declining-issue line was aimed upward and the advancing-issue line was pointing downward. These lines were forecasting a period in the near future with 1400–1500 declining issues, which is a massacre.

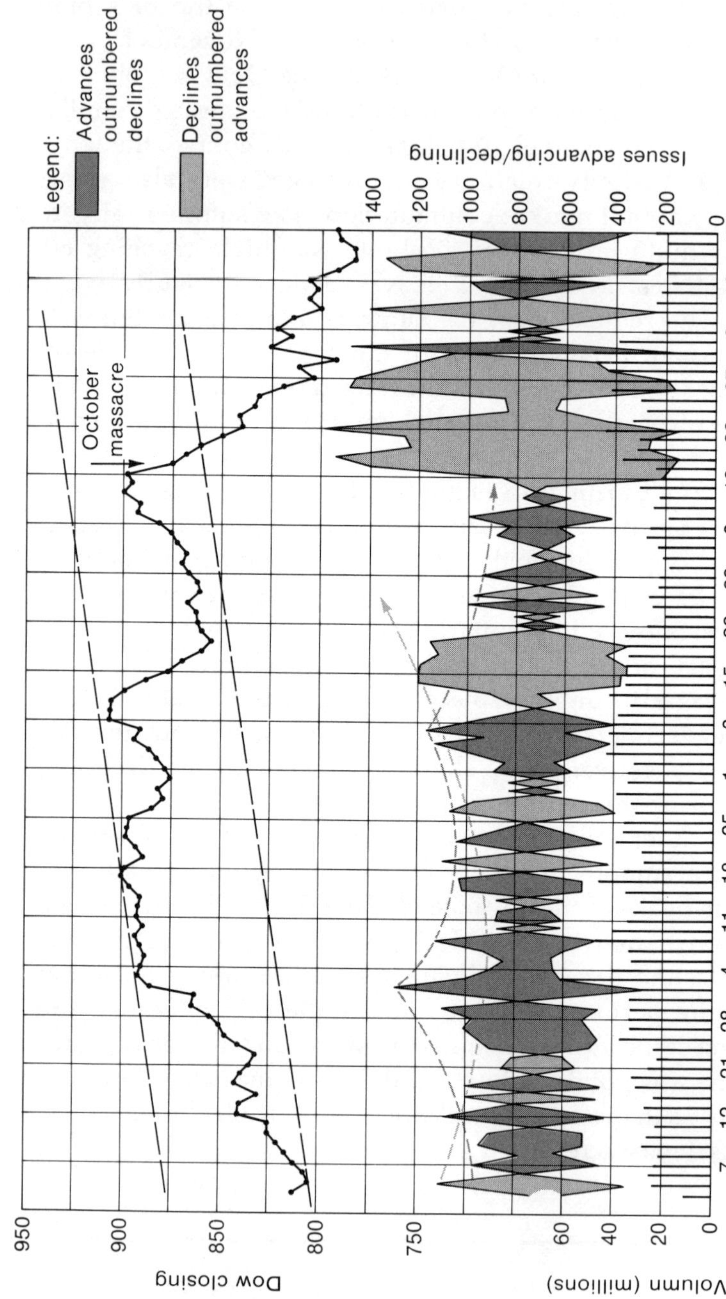

FIGURE 6.3. The daily pulse of the NYSE, Jul.–Nov. 1978

Guidelines for Interpreting the Daily Pulse

Following is a set of simple, clear guidelines for interpreting the data that you collect on the daily pulse chart for each exchange.

Indications of an impending massacre or bear market are:

- a bull market has been in progress for a long time and,
- the market average is recovering from a correction, and
- the recovery is occurring on low volume and,
- the number of advancing issues is only slightly higher than the number of declining issues and,
- the line connecting the peaks of declining issues is sloped upward.

Indications of an impending bull market are:

- a bear market has been in progress for a long time and,
- the line connecting the peaks of advancing issues is sloped upward and,
- the number of declining issues is only slightly higher than the number of advancing issues when the market average retreats and,
- the number of advancing issues is substantially higher than the number of declining issues when the market average advances.

This concludes the part of the book concerned with monitoring market averages. In the next part, we will look more closely at the stocks you will be buying and selling, and at how to make objective decisions based on the data you've charted in this part.

Your Action Steps

- Draw any obvious trend lines on your moving averages chart for each exchange; be on the alert for trend lines and channels that may be developing.
- Set up a daily pulse chart for each exchange, with data for at least the past month.
- Begin plotting daily close data each evening on these charts.
- Watch the daily pulse for configurations that would alert you to impending changes in market direction.

Part III

THE STOCKS

Chapter 7

DEVELOPING YOUR RESERVOIR OF STOCKS

In previous chapters we have discussed the market. Once you have in place the system described for monitoring the NYSE and the Amex, the day will come when all the signals tell you that a bear market is over and that you must buy stocks to make money in the coming bull market. Then you will be faced with deciding which stocks to buy. This chapter will show you how to

- select a reservoir of stocks from which to buy and sell
- collect data about the stocks in your reservoir, upon which to base your buying and selling decisions

Selecting the Stocks

The time to begin thinking about which stocks to buy at the bottom of a bear market is months in advance. The more historical data you have upon which to base your buying and selling decisions, the more sound those decisions will be. It's very helpful to have data on the behavior of a number of stocks through several bear and bull markets. With this kind of long-term information, you can select a tentative portfolio and formulate a buying plan long before the bottom of a bear market occurs.

An essential part of this system is a reservoir of about two hundred stocks, on each of which you should have about two years' worth of information. When it comes time to buy, you will consult your data about the stocks in your reservoir and make decisions accordingly.

Many of the stocks in my reservoir have been there for at least ten years. I own some of them at this time. Some of them I have bought and sold numerous times during the last twenty years. Some I have never bought, and maybe never will.

Most of the companies whose stocks I have chosen to include in my reservoir are manufacturers of nice down-to-earth products like women's handbags, screws and fasteners, diapers, paint, auto parts, and housing products. I chose to include many of these stocks in my reservoir because at the time they were chosen, they were definitely underpriced, particularly with regard to book value and potential future earnings. Many stocks have been removed from my reservoir because they have been taken over by other companies. From time to time, I add some new stocks to my reservoir to replace those removed. In Appendix A you will find a list of the stocks in my reservoir. You might want to turn to it and read it over before you are told how to select your own reservoir.

If you have been following the stock market for long, you probably already have a few stocks whose performances you've been watching. You may own some of these stocks, or you may not. Whatever the case, now is the time to become much more systematic about tracking their performances. You should pick out twenty-five or so companies on which to begin keeping data sheets, and you should add a few more to your reservoir each month until you have a number you feel is manageable, but at least one hundred. The stocks in your reservoir should include those you already follow, stocks in industries that appeal to you, stocks in the price range you like, and stocks in industries that you think have a good future. You might also want to include some of the stocks that are in my reservoir.

Collecting Data About Your Stocks

To start collecting data about your stocks, obtain from your broker the Standard and Poor's (S&P) data sheets for about twenty-five of the stocks you decide to include in your reservoir. If you are a relatively good customer, he or she should comply without hesitation. It will take you a fair amount of time to bring these up to date so twenty-five is more than enough for the first step. After you have these up to date, request ten to fifteen more per week until you have filled your reservoir.

When you request the S&P sheets, do not request the originals. In most cases your broker won't send these anyway because they usually have only one copy on hand. Specifically request copies of the sheet. It is helpful if they have a copier that will duplex; you will have only one sheet copied front and back rather than one sheet for the front and one for the back of the S&P sheet. Furthermore, request that the copy *not* be centered but rather that the S&P sheet be positioned in the top left of the copy sent to you. This will place a big margin on the right which will be used as described later for weekly updating of the market performance data on the company's stock. Punch holes in these data sheets and place them in your binder behind a new divider labelled "Reservoir of Stocks."

The S&P sheets give a reasonable description of the company's business. You should carefully read this description now, and periodically reread it. You should underline salient features. For example, if it looks like housing should start to pick up in the next few months and the company has a stake in some phase of the housing market, this item should be underlined as a positive. On the other hand, if housing is expected to decline because of tight money or some other factor, underline any exposure to the housing market as a negative. This is important information if you are considering buying this stock. Personally, I underline positives in green and negatives in red. This makes the item stand out in future readings of the sheet. Circle such things as unusually high dividend rate, very high book value, high depreciation, high current assets to debits, etc. These items can signal an underpriced stock.

The most important data on the sheet are the quarterly tabulation of the sales and earnings, and the plot of the monthly stock prices and volume. The only problem with this data is that it will be out of date. In fact, as much as six months' worth of recent data might be missing. Since this data is vital, the charts and earning data must be brought up to date. *Barron's* is the best source for this information. If you don't have a subscription, you should be able to get back copies from your broker or a large public library. If neither of the above is possible then you must start to update the data as described below and contend for a few months with a gap in your chart.

Some brokers don't subscribe to Standard & Poor's, or might be reluctant to give you copies of sheets because of the cost. (They are copyrighted and the broker must pay a fee for every copy made.) If they do not subscribe to S&P, they probably subscribe to Moody's Investor's Service. These sheets contain information similar to the S&P sheets. There is only one difficulty with these sheets; they are a full 8½″ × 11″ in size, leaving you no space to tabulate the weekly performance data of the stocks on the front of your copy. You could copy it onto legal size paper, which gives a large space at the bottom for data.

Keeping S&P or Moody's Sheets Up to Date

A weekly summary of the performance of all stocks on the NYSE and the Amex is given in either the Saturday or Sunday edition of many major newspapers. If it is not in your paper, then you will have to obtain it from *Barron's* on Monday. It is particularly helpful if these data are in your Saturday paper; you then have the entire weekend to record the data and to study it in preparation for decisions to buy or sell in the coming week. This is particularly important near the tops or bottoms of bull markets. Note, this weekly update of the stocks in your reservoir is entered directly onto the S&P or Moody's sheets so all the information on any one stock is in one place. An example of the front of one of my old sheets is shown in Figure 7.1. It is not pretty but then it isn't supposed to be; it is a work sheet. The right hand column of handwritten numbers consists of the low price of the week, the high price of the week, and the closing price for the week for the given stock. In parentheses is the number of shares of stock traded that week. A line is drawn to separate one week's data from the next's. These weekly data are the source for updating the chart in the right-hand column of the S&P sheet, which is the history of the performance of this stock. The chart is important because trend lines can be drawn on it and trigger buy or sell signals. You will learn more about this in the next chapter.

The monthly chart must be kept up to date. Since it is almost impossible to obtain data that covers an exact calendar month, the best alternative is to use four- and five-week months for plotting the data. For example, in March 1979 the Thursday and Friday data for March 1 and 2 is included in the last weekly data for February, rather than in the March data. This monthly chart is kept up to date weekly. After the first week of a new month, the range of price and volume for the week is entered. In subsequent weeks, the lines are extended.

Eventually, as is the case with the example sheet, you will run out of space to record data. You must obtain a new sheet from your broker. This sheet will be partly out of date, so transfer all missing late data on earnings, etc., from the old to

Westinghouse Electric

2470

NYSE Symbol WX Options on ASE

Price	Range	P-E Ratio	Dividend	Yield	S&P Ranking
Jul. 26'79	1979				
20¼	21-16½	5	0.972	4.8%	B+

Summary

Westinghouse Electric is the second largest manufacturer of electrical equipment and the leader in nuclear power equipment. Auditors qualified their opinion of WX's 1978 financial statements subject to the resolution of uncertainties arising from lawsuits by electric utilities alleging breach of uranium supply contracts. While ongoing businesses should show long-term progress, further possible settlements of lawsuits are likely to involve significant payments by Westinghouse.

Current Outlook

If the strike which began July 16 ends quickly, earnings for 1979 (excluding charges related to uranium supply contracts litigation) could reach $4.00 a share or more, up from 1978's $3.59 (before $0.78 special charges).

Dividends may remain at $0.243 quarterly until the uncertainties arising from the litigation are clarified.

Aided by expansion in capital spending, the Industry Products group will likely show good earnings improvement in 1979. The Public Systems group should also show further progress, helped by improvement in nonresidential construction and defense business. Power Systems group profits may rise only slightly, due to lackluster prospects for generation equipment.

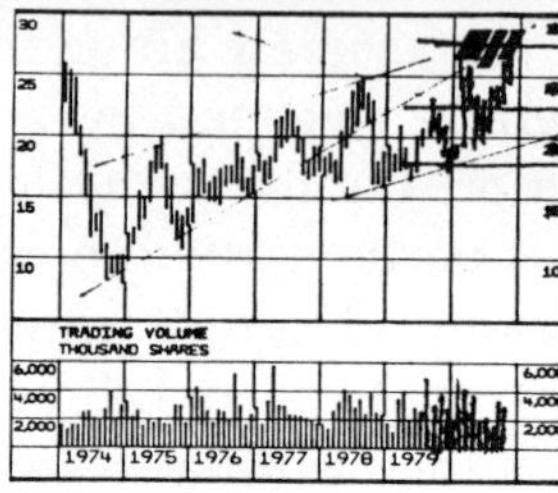

Net Sales (Million $)

Quarter:	1979	1978	1977	1976
Mar.	1,782	1,545	1,428	1,443
Jun.	1,921	1,677	1,533	1,551
Sep.		1,659	1,514	1,467
Dec.		1,783	1,663	1,684
		6,663	6,138	6,145

First half 1979 sales rose 14.9%. Net income was up 23.5%. Share earnings equaled $2.02 (before $1.97 special charges), versus $1.62.

Common Share Earnings ($)

Quarter:	1979	[3]1978	[3]1977	1976
Mar.	0.96	0.76	0.66	0.54
Jun.	1.06	0.86	0.73	0.62
Sep.		0.95	0.82	0.67
Dec.		1.02	0.89	0.71
		3.59	3.10	2.54

Important Developments

Jul. 16'79—Three unions representing 37,500 employees went on strike as their labor contracts expired.

Jun. '79—As of June 30, 1979 the 10 settlements reached with public utility customers (who charged Westinghouse with breach of uranium supply contracts) represented over 55% of the total uranium originally claimed by all of the plaintiffs. The 10 settlements have resulted in a cumulative extraordinary loss of $497.8 million before taxes, and $260.5 million after taxes. Losses (after taxes) in the first half of 1979 were $170 million ($1.97 a share).

Next earnings report due in mid-October.

Per Share Data ($)

Yr. End Dec. 31	1978	1977	1976	1975	1974	1973	[1]1972	[1]1971	[1]1970	[1]1969
Book Value	27.46	25.54	23.54	21.88	20.83	21.33	20.59	19.20	16.79	16.40
Earnings[2]	3.59	3.10	2.54	2.04	1.57	1.82	2.24	2.08	1.53	1.88
Dividends	0.97¼	0.97¼	0.97¼	0.97¼	0.97¼	0.97¼	0.93⅝	0.90	0.90	0.90
Payout Ratio	27%	31%	38%	48%	61%	53%	42%	45%	59%	48%
Prices—High	25	22¼	19½	20	26	47⅜	54⅞	48⅞	34⅞	35⅝
Low	16	16¼	13	9¾	8	24¼	38⅜	32⅝	26⅝	26¾
P/E Ratio—	7-4	7-5	8-5	10-5	17-5	26-13	24-17	23-16	23-17	19-14

Data as orig. reptd. Adj. for stk. div(s). of 100% Dec. 1971. 1. Reflects merger or acquisition. 2. Bef. results of disc. opers. of −0.15 in 1975, −1.26 in 1974, and spec. item(s) of −0.78 in 1978, −0.24 in 1977. 3. Bef. extraordinary losses.

Standard NYSE Stock Reports Vol. 46/No. 149/Sec. 16

August 2, 1979

Standard & Poor's Corp. 345 Hudson St., NY, NY 10014

FIGURE 7.1. S&P sheet with data up to date

the new sheet. Likewise, you will have to update the monthly chart on the new sheet. Keep at least one month's worth of the latest weekly data on the new S&P sheet. After a stock split, you will also need to obtain a new sheet.

This may all sound very time consuming, but it is not. Recording and plotting the data for my reservoir of stocks takes me about an hour and a half every weekend. The data should also be *studied* carefully for buy or sell signals or unusual volume activity. Besides plotting weekly data on your S&P or Moody's sheets, you should examine the earnings digest section of the *Wall Street Journal* daily to see if there are any new earnings reports on the stocks in your reservoir. If so, you must update the sales and earnings tables on the S&P or Moody's sheets. Increasing sales is a sign of a growing company. Likewise, as will be seen in the next chapter, you will use any new earnings report to calculate the latest 12 month's earnings and estimated book value and new Index of Merit for your stock. You should also examine the dividend section of the *Wall Street Journal* to see if there are any changes for the stocks in your reservoir. An increase in dividend is bullish for a stock. If there is a change, you should enter it at the top of your sheet, as shown in the example. If a stock has gone ex-dividend, indicate it by an asterisk before your weekly data. You may also want to clip and save any news item that pertains to your stocks.

Evaluating Long-Term Information

The S&P or Moody's sheets are valuable for keeping near-term information on a stock up to date. In addition, they provide much valuable long-term data such as historical price, earnings, and dividends for the last ten years. They also provide information on the number of shares outstanding, debt, depreciation, etc. Just about all the information pertinent to the price value of a stock will be there on your up-to-date S&P or Moody's sheet.

One of the most important pieces of information to you about a stock is its historical price/earnings (P/E) ratio. A low P/E ratio in comparison to other stocks is not necessarily a good criterion for buying a stock. Only by comparing the present P/E ratio of a stock with its own historic high and low P/E ratios can you decide if it would be a good investment. For instance, at a P/E of 9, IBM is low, but at a P/E of 6, many textile stocks are high.

Now that you have learned how to keep an up-to-date record on each stock in a reservoir you have chosen, your next step will be to learn when to buy and sell based on your data. The next chapter covers this topic.

Your Action Steps

- Select initially at least twenty-five stocks for your reservoir.
- Obtain copies of S&P or Moody's sheets on the selected stocks.
- Use back issues of *Barron's* to bring these sheets up to date.
- Each weekend, record on each S&P or Moody's sheet the weekly high, low, and closing price of the stock and the volume of stock traded that week.
- Plot the data on the graph that appears on the S&P or Moody's sheet.
- Scan the *Wall Street Journal* daily for new earnings reports or dividend changes, and record them on the S&P or Moody's sheets.
- Select an additional ten or fifteen stocks each week until you have at least one hundred stocks in your reservoir.

Chapter 8

TIMING YOUR STOCK TRANSACTIONS

Now we come to the critical question of when to buy and when to sell a specific stock. When a bear market is over, how can you tell if an individual stock is at a low price? When a bull market is progressing, how can you tell when an individual stock is at a high price and should be sold? When a bull market is in progress, how can you tell when an individual stock is still at a low price and should be bought? In this chapter two methods will be shown for timing your stock market transactions:

- using the Index of Merit
- using trend lines and channels for individual stocks

Using the Index of Merit

You will recall that one of the premises of this system is that stocks are usually not priced at their fair value; almost always they are either underpriced or overpriced. Obviously, you want to buy them when they are substantially underpriced and sell them when they are slightly overpriced. If you buy when a stock is only slightly underpriced, your risk is high and your potential profit is low. Likewise, if you wait for a stock to become substantially overpriced, you have a high risk of losing your profit.

The statistic that is calculated in this system for each stock in your reservoir to show whether it is currently overpriced or underpriced is called the Index of Merit. Essentially the Index of Merit for a stock is an estimate of its fair value. When the price of a stock drops a certain number of percentage points below the Index of Merit, it is a prime candidate for buying. Similarly, when the price of the stock rises to or slightly surpasses the Index of Merit, the stock is a prime candidate for selling.

Various formulas were used to calculate an index of merit and tested on several hundred stocks over the period from 1975 to 1981. The formula given below was found to be the most satisfactory for predicting good buying and selling points for most stocks. If a bear market has ended, it is a profitable strategy to buy stocks that are priced 70 percent or more below their Index of Merit and to sell these stocks when they reach their Index of Merit.

Calculating the Index of Merit

The formula for calculating the Index of Merit is as follows:

- Index of Merit = (.5 × book value) + (1.75 × last twelve months' earnings) + annual depreciation + annual change in earnings

If you will look at your S&P or Moody's sheets for your individual stocks, you will see that you have all the information needed for this calculation.

- The current book value will be an approximation except for the end-of-the-year data. The quarterly earnings minus the dividend is an estimate of the quarterly increase in the book value. This number is added to the last book value to obtain the current book value.
- The last twelve months' earnings is simply the sum of the earnings for the last four quarters.
- Depreciation is reported annually. Therefore, the value reported at year end is used throughout the following year.
- Annual change in earnings is the difference between the current annual earnings and the annual earnings of one year ago.

Every time a new earnings report is issued for one of the stocks in your reservoir, you will need to recalculate the Index of Merit and the buy point.

You can set up a table to organize your data and to calculate the Index of Merit on the back of your S&P or Moody's sheet for each stock. It should look like Table 8.1. The Index of Merit for March 1980 for this stock was calculated as follows:

Increase in book value = (earnings of .65) – (dividend of .30) = .35

TABLE 8.1. Table for Organizing Data and Calculating Index of Merit

DATE	QUARTERLY EARNINGS	EARNINGS LAST 12 MO	DIVIDEND	BOOK VALUE	DEPRECIATION	INDEX OF MERIT	BUY POINT
1978 Dec.	.60	2.00	.25	14.00	1.00		
1979 Mar.	.55	2.15	.25	14.30			
June	.55	2.30	.25	14.60			
Sept.	.70	2.40	.25	15.05			
Dec.	.65	2.45	.30	15.40	1.10	13.54	9.48
1980 Mar.	.65	2.55	.30	15.75		13.84	9.69
June	.60	2.60	.30	16.05		13.98	9.79
Sept.	.80	2.70	.30	16.55		14.40	10.08
Dec.	.75	2.80	.35	16.95	1.20	14.93	10.45

March book value = (December book value of 15.40) + (increase of .35) = 15.75.

.5 × book value = .5 × 15.75 + 7.88

Last twelve months' earnings = .55 + .70 + .65 + .65 = 2.55

1.75 × last twelve months' earnings = 1.75 × 2.55 = 4.46

The latest reported depreciation is 1.10.

Change in earnings = (March 1980 earnings of 2.55) − (March 1979 earnings of 2.15) = .40.

The Index of Merit can now be calculated:

Index = 7.88 + 4.46 + 1.10 + .40 = 13.84

The buy point for the next quarter is obtained by multiplying the index by 0.7.

Buy point = 13.84 × 0.7 = 9.69

The data are plotted in Figure 8.1. The book value and the Index of Merit calculated from the earnings report of December 1979 are plotted at the December 1979 point. The buy point calculated from this data, however, is plotted at the March 1980 point because it is the buy point for the current quarter already in progress. The range of the price of the stock each quarter is also plotted on this chart. If the stock's price should fall below 10⅝ during the quarter ending March 31, it should be bought. If you own the stock and the price should go above 15½ it should be sold. The December 1979 data in Figure 8.1 is particularly interesting in that it includes the October 1979 massacre. The price of the stock dropped to 8, which was well below the buy point at that time. Subsequent prices for this stock certainly proved it was underpriced.

After several years, you will have enough historical data to calculate a more precise buy point for your stocks than the

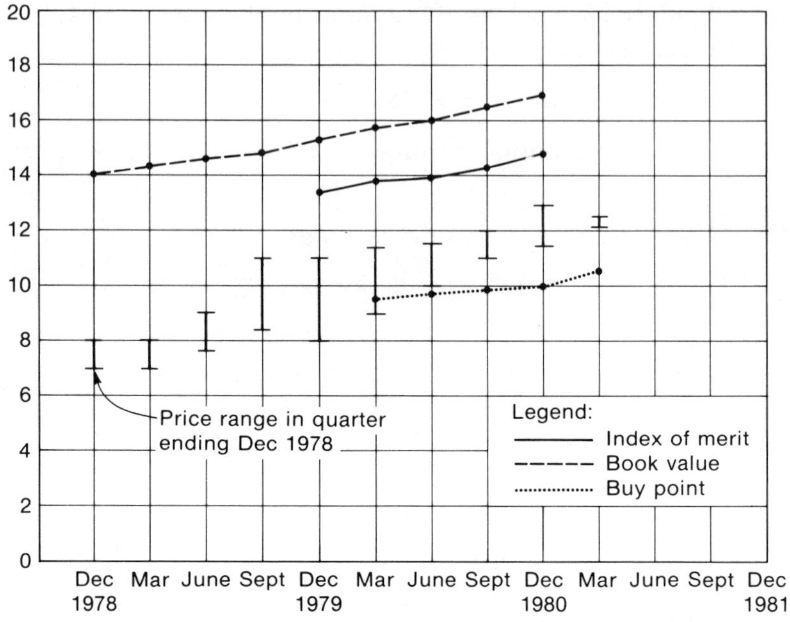

FIGURE 8.1. Chart of Index of Merit data

general 70 percent. The 70 percent buy point is a good value to use when you start following a stock. If, however, over several years the price of a stock has gone as high as its Index of Merit at least once a year but has never gone below 80 percent of the Index of Merit, then you should use 80 percent to calculate the buy point for this stock in the future. On the other hand, if the price of a stock has frequently gone down to 40 percent of its Index of Merit, then the buy point for this stock should be 40 percent of the Index of Merit; the sell point for such a stock might well be only 70 percent of the Index of Merit.

For a given stock, it is apparent that the lower the buy point is set, the greater the safety of the investment. But, of course, the lower the buy point is set, the fewer the number of stocks that will become candidates for purchase and the greater the number of good buying opportunities that will be missed. The same reasoning applies on the sell side. The ultraconservative investor might sell when a stock reaches 90 percent of the Index of Merit whereas the more aggressive investor will wait until the price is 120 percent of the Index of Merit. The following case histories illustrate the use of the Index of Merit.

CASE HISTORY: Using the index of merit to buy and sell stock in Fab Industries

In December 1974 the stock of this company was the steal of the century. It was priced at 75¢ per share. Its book value was $5.64. Earnings were down to only 27¢ per share from 57¢ the previous year but even so, the P/E was still only 3. If an investor bought 1000 shares for $750 the maximum loss, if the company went completely bankrupt, would be only $750. But the potential profits, if the price of the stock returned to its former high of 19, would be $18,000. The Index of Merit at that time was 3½ and the 70 percent buy point was at 2½. The Standard and Poor's chart on this company showed that it had reached a high of 14½ in 1970.

Figure 8.2 shows the performance of this company's stock and the Index of Merit data for the period from November 1977 to November 1981. During this period the price of the stock reached the buy point (70 percent of index) many times. Between November 1977 and May 1978, purchases could have been made between 4½ and 5⅜. A sell signal occurred in September 1978 when the price exceeded the Index of Merit. The entire position in this stock could have been sold at about 9 for a profit of about 80 percent. This sale would have turned to gold, however, because the October 1978 massacre occurred shortly thereafter and the investor would have been holding cash. The price dropped during the massacre to almost 6, which was close enough to the buy point to again start buying the stock.

The year-end report of November 1978 showed a tremendous increase in earnings and therefore a large increase in

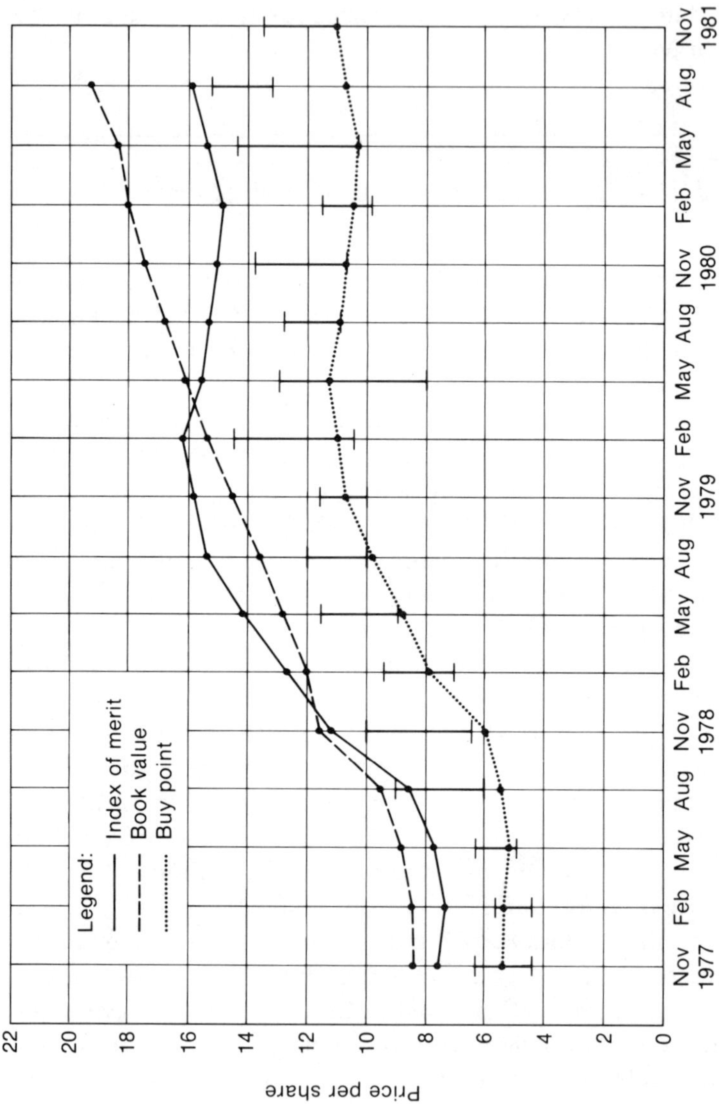

FIGURE 8.2. *Performance of Fab Industries stock and its Index of Merit*

the Index of Merit and a much higher buy point. Yet the stock could still be bought below 8, which was the buy point for early 1979. Throughout 1979, there were buying opportunities. Even the October 1979 massacre was not too devastating for this stock.

In January 1980 the price surged to over 14. The price was still not up to the Index of Merit but the quarterly top price over the long term for this stock was historically always lower than the corresponding quarterly Index of Merit. Furthermore, it was apparent that the slope of the Index of Merit wasn't increasing as fast as it had been; the investor could have sold for almost 100 percent profits at this point, and would have done so if prudent. Again, this sale would have proven even better than expected because within a few weeks, the February 1980 massacre hit the market and by early March the price of this stock was down to 8. At 8, the price was well below the buy point.

From June 1980 to March 1981, the price of this stock was frequently below the buy point and an aggressive purchase program should have been followed. In May 1981, the price again approached the Index of Merit and selling should have started at about 14 for a profit of about 35 percent. The entire position should have been sold before August of 1981 at prices as high as 15. Again, these sales would have put the investor into cash before the bear market of 1981.

CASE HISTORY: Using the index of merit to buy and sell stock in Grand Auto

The performance of this company's stock since late 1978 has been a trader's dream come true. See Figure 8.3. In August 1978 this stock could have been bought at between 7½ and 8, with a buy point of 8. In September 1978, the price reached 11½, which was close enough to the Index of Merit to warrant selling for a 44 percent profit. This sale had the unexpected bonus of getting the investor into cash just before the October 1978 massacre. During the next three months, the stock could

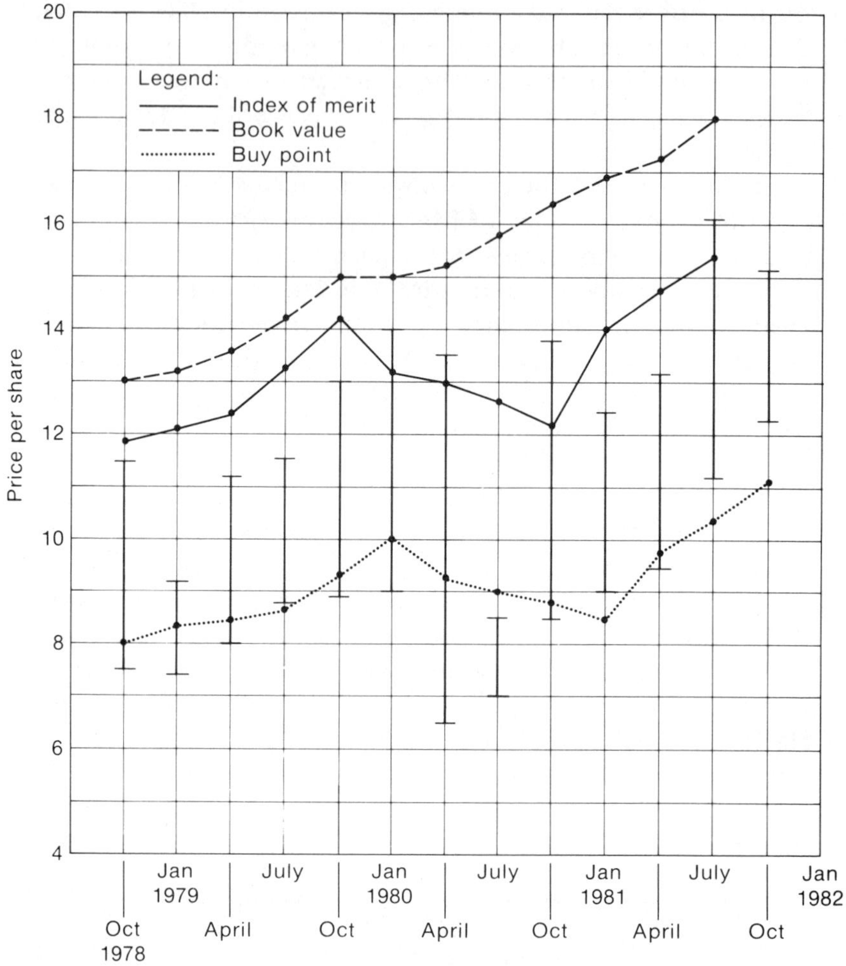

FIGURE 8.3. Performance of Grand Auto stock and its Index of Merit

have been bought back in the buy zone between 7½ and 8¼. Every quarter until January 1980 offered the opportunity to buy and sell this stock at least once for a profit of about 33 percent each quarter.

During the March 1980 massacre, the price of this stock dropped to a low of 6½, far below its buy point of 9¼. By the rules, the investor should have started buying this stock at 9¼. However, the prudent investor might have taken into consideration that the Index of Merit was in a downtrend at that time and used a 60 percent buy criterion rather than the 70 percent criterion. This would have restricted buys to less than 8 during the period from March to August 1980. These purchases would have paid off in September 1980 when the price of the stock went above the Index of Merit at about 12½. Profits were at least 55 percent.

In February 1981, the price of this stock was again in the buy zone below 9¾ and reached the Index of Merit at 15½ in June for another 50 percent profit. Again, an investor would have obtained the added bonus of missing the 1981 bear market that started in August.

CASE HISTORY: Using the Index of Merit to buy and sell stock in Jaclyn

This case, depicted in Figure 8.4, is interesting for several reasons. The stock's buy point was 80 percent of the Index of Merit because it had never reached the 70 percent buy point. For three years starting in the quarter ending December 1978, this stock hit its buy point in every quarter. Through 1979 and most of 1980 this stock could have been bought at about 4½. It reached and surpassed its Index of Merit (6) for a profit of 33 percent just before the December 1980 massacre. Every quarter thereafter, this stock has reached the buy point and the Index of Merit (almost) for a trading profit of 20 to 25 percent per quarter. Because of its high book value, a stock such as this is a prime candidate for a takeover.

CASE HISTORY: Using the Index of Merit to buy and sell stock in Maul Technology

Figure 8.5 shows the performance of this stock in relationship to its Index of Merit and the conventional 70 percent buy

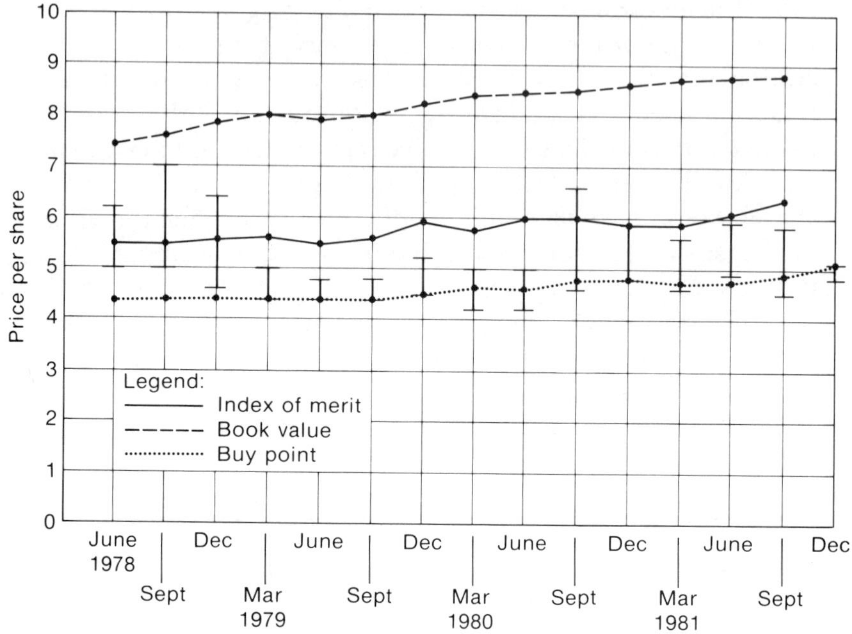

FIGURE 8.4. Performance of Jaclyn stock and its Index of Merit

point. The Index of Merit for this stock was flat at about 3, but the price stayed above the Index of Merit until the June 1979 quarter. Earning data for that quarter showed a sharp turnaround from six previous dismal quarters. The first buy opportunity occurred after the 1979 massacre when the price dropped to 3¼. A buying opportunity occurred in almost every quarter thereafter through March 1981. Selling opportunities as defined by the Index of Merit likewise occurred in either the same or next quarter for profits of about 50 percent per quarter. The final surge in the price to 8⅝ in the last part of 1981 resulted from a takeover offer at 9.

In the above case histories, you can see that most of these stocks reached the Index of Merit, or were very close to it, just

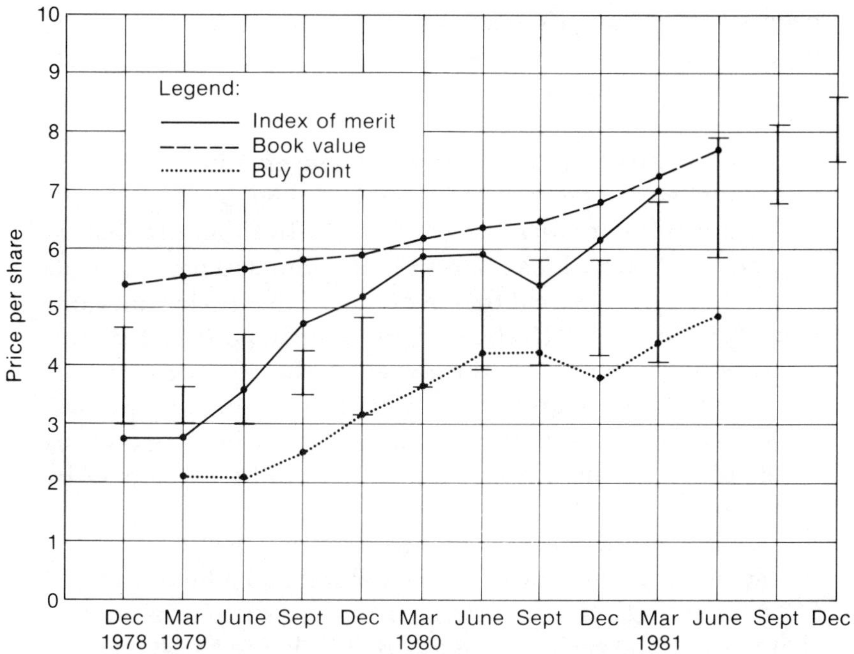

FIGURE 8.5. Performance of Maul Technology stock and its Index of Merit

prior to massacres. This behavior has been observed in many stocks other than these. Selling stock when it reaches the Index of Merit is one of the best protections against massacres.

The Index of Merit and a $9000 Investment in 1976

To test how an investor could have done during the period 1976–80 using the Index of Merit and the 70 percent buying rule, I chose the first six stocks from the Amex that were in my portfolio in January 1976 and applied the rules for buying and selling with a postulated initial investment of less than $9000. At certain times during the period, profits could have been taken in one of the stocks while none of the others was in a buy zone, so it is presumed that these funds lay idle for various periods of time. Table 8.2 is a tabulation of the transactions.

The investor who used the most conservative of buy and sell points would have as of December 1980, $51,000 in cash and a portfolio of stocks worth $17,000 from an original investment of $9000. This is a return of about 740 percent in six years. It will be apparent that over half of the total profit came from the sale of NSN (National Spinning). In January 1981 this stock was dropped from the Amex as the company officers bought up all the shares at 12 and took the company private. This was no surprise; one should expect at least one of six companies that one buys by this system to be taken over by someone.

At the end of the 1978 massacre, stock in this company was selling for 3 in spite of the fact that it had a book value of $12.48, earnings of 88¢ a share, and depreciation of $1.30 a share, for a total cash flow of $2.18. It Index of Merit was 7.8. Even in 1980 you could buy the shares at about 5, which was still a steal.

Using Trend Lines and Channels

Just as market averages tend to trend upward or downward while fluctuating within certain recognizable channels, so too do individual stock prices. If you are willing to watch prices of the stocks in your reservoir more closely and to do trading at shorter intervals, you can use trend lines and channels as well as the Index of Merit to alert you to buying and selling opportunities. If you don't have the time or the inclination, you can still do well basing your buying decisions on the Index of Merit only.

If you want to use this optional method, draw trend lines on your S&P or Moody's charts for your individual stocks in the same manner as you drew them on your market average

TABLE 8.2. Hypothetical Performance of the Index of Merit, 1976–1980

YEAR	STOCK	PURCHASES	SALES	PROFIT IN CASH
1975	CRW	$1475		
	FIT	725		
	FTM	100	$ 300	
	INS	6500		
		8800	300	
1976	CRW	650	3500	
	FTM	100		
	INS	1850		
	NSN	275		
		2875	3500	$ 600
1977	BLX	350		
	FIT	725		
	FTM	550		
	NSN	5350		
	INS	–	13,300	
		6975	13,300	6000
1978	BLX	325		
	FIT	1525	5000	
	FTM	2250	5400	
	NSN	2250		
	INS	–	5400	
		6350	15,800	9500
1979	BLX	700		
	FIT	2400		
	FTM	350		
	NSN	4100		
	INS	–	4800	
		7550	4800	-3000
1980	BLX	1775		
	FIT	800	5600	
	FTM	2025		
	INS	450		
	NSN	–	38,000	
		5050	43,600	38,000

charts. The idea is that when a bull market is in progress, you will want to buy stocks when their prices decline to the lower trend line, and sell stocks when their prices rise to the upper trend line. Let's look at a few case histories to see how this works.

CASE HISTORY: *Using trend lines and channels to buy and sell stock in U.S. Industries*

Some facts on the company in December 1974: it was highly diversified and was in apparel, building, industrial services and leisure markets; between 1968 and 1973, it had earned between \$1.75 and \$2.17 per share per year; it had a book value of almost \$13 per share; in 1968 it had sold as high as \$35; as late as 1973 it had sold for \$21 a share; the dividend was 65¢ a share; its price on the NYSE in December 1973 was 7.

Both the NYSE and the Amex were in typical bear market configurations throughout 1974. The price of U.S. Industries was also in a bear market mode (see Figure 8.6). There was justification for the bear market in this stock; the earning figures at the top of Figure 8.6 indicate that the company was having a problem making money. In June 1974 quarterly earnings were only 37¢ per share and the price of the stock dropped to 5. Then the September earning: only 14¢ a share and the price of the stock dropped to 3. It could be expected that January's earnings would be even worse. It appeared in October and November that this company would soon be out of business, and the price of the stock dropped to 2 in December 1974.

In fact, investors were overlooking positive aspects of the company. First, the finances of this company were sound and very few companies with sales of a billion and a half go completely broke so that their stock becomes worthless. Second, at one time some investors thought that the company was worth \$35 a share; at \$2 a share most of its problems must

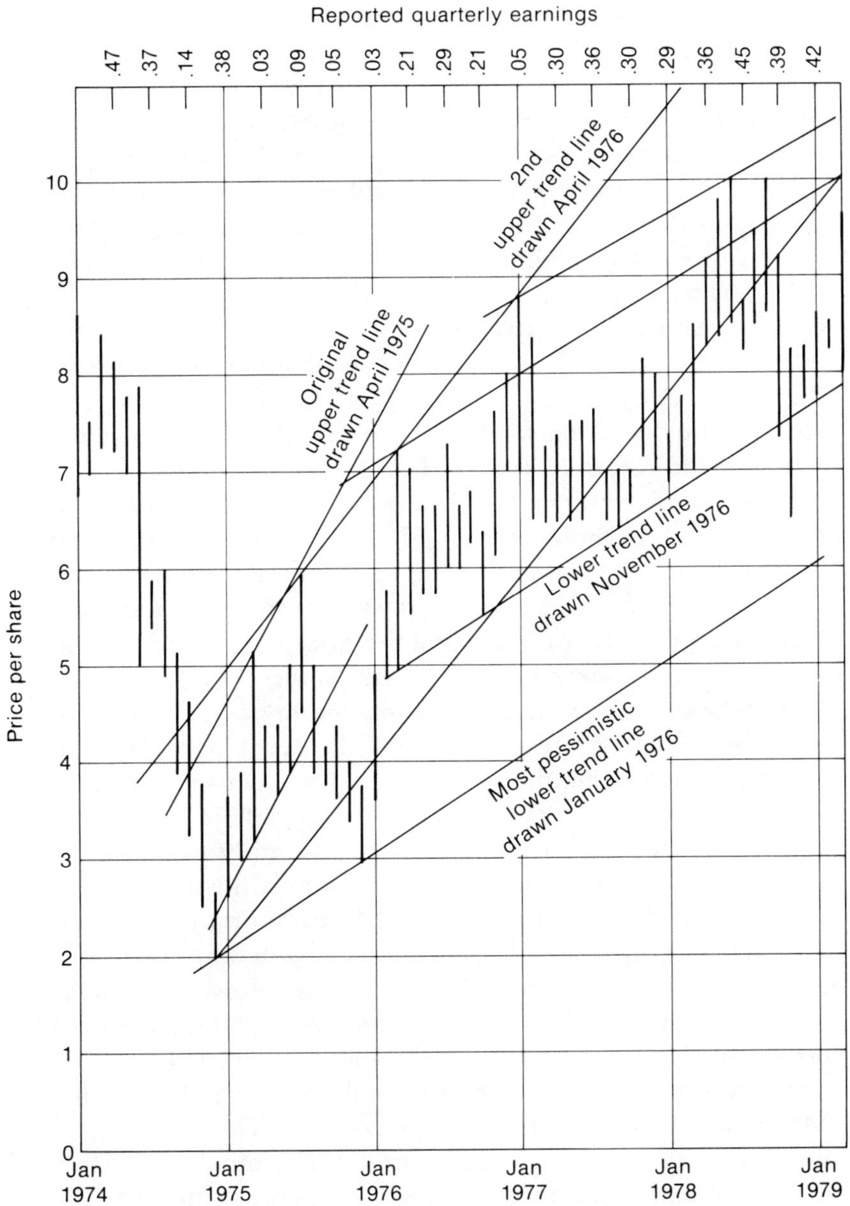

FIGURE 8.6. *Performance of U.S. Industries stock and its trend lines*

have already been discounted. Third, with a book value of $12.79 the stock was selling at only 16 percent of book; certainly one should have been able to recover a major part of an investment in this company if it went out of business. Fourth, with a dividend of 56¢ per share, the stock was paying 28 percent; even if the dividend were cut in half, it would still be paying 14 percent. Fifth, depreciation was over $1 per year; even without any earnings this was substantial cash flow for a stock selling at $2.

Now all these positives were also present in August, for example, but the price of the stock continued to fall. Why was this a good stock to buy in December when it was not a good stock to buy in August? The answer is that in August the pressure indicators of the market all pointed down; in December the indicators were showing the first signs of a turnaround in the whole market. If the market did turn and become a bull market and if the economy did improve then surely U.S. Industries would solve its problems and start making a lot of money again and the price of the stock would go up. An investment in 1000 shares would only cost, at the most, $2500, which would be the maximum possible loss. On the other hand, if the price eventually went only to book value, the profit potential was over $10,000. Let us assume that an investor made this purchase in December 1974.

In January and February 1975, the monthly range of the stock price plotted on the chart makes it look like the decision to purchase this stock was brilliant. More important, however, was that performance of the stock was generating valuable information. In early April 1975 the monthly lows of January, February, and March were connected with a straight line to establish a lower trend line. Furthermore, an upper trend line could be established through the peak for the high price for March and parallel to the lower trend line. The lower trend line was verified in May and June. In July, the price of this stock was almost up to the upper trend line. Without question, one should have started selling at about 5½ and been completely sold out at 5¾.

Another bad earning report for June came out and the price of the stock dropped to the lower trend line in August; not only did it hit the lower trend line but it went through it decisively. The September earnings report was bad and didn't help the stock price. During this period, our investor would probably have started buying at about 4¼ and continued to buy in, say, 100 share lots down to 3. Actually the company's prospects looked good. Even if the company only broke even in the December quarterly earnings report, it would look good compared to the December quarter previous, when the company lost 38¢ per share.

In January 1976 a new most pessimistic lower trend line was established through the lows of December 1974 and December 1975. In March 1976 as the price approached 7 it was also approaching the original upper trend line and selling should have commenced and been completed at about 6¾. The April performance confirmed a new upper trend line connecting the July 1975 and the March 1976 highs. The lower trend line could not be drawn until November 1976; this lower trend line is parallel to the upper line and through the December 1974 and the October 1976 lows. Actually, in November it was possible to draw the lower trend line through the lows of February, March, and October 1976 and an upper trend line parallel to this through the high of March 1976. This channel stayed in effect through 1979. A short-term trader would have been justified in rebuying U.S. Industries stock in October and November at 5½ to 6½ and selling out at about 7½ in December and January as the price approached the upper trend line.

In September 1977 the price of the stock stopped exactly on the lower trend line and this stock should again have been bought at about 6½. The validity of the lower trend line was repeatedly confirmed throughout 1977 and 1978, and additional buying at prices up to 7 would have been advised. In April 1978 the price approached the upper trend line and selling at about 9 was prudent even though the price eventually reached 10. Then came the October 1978 massacre; at

7½ the stock was at the lower trend line and buying should have commenced even though the price eventually dropped to 6½.

A partial selling in March 1979 and a complete sellout by August 1979 at over 10 were all dictated by the upper trend line which had been in effect since March 1976. Actually a nimble trader could have bought and sold several times in 1979. There was absolutely no reason for an intelligent investor to have been caught in the October 1979 massacre holding any U.S. Industries stock. Finally, at the end of the October massacre, the buy signal of the lower trend line again flashed green for this stock.

It should be noted that if an investor had been using the Index of Merit with this stock, it would have been bought in early and late 1975 at about 3 and would have been sold in early 1977 at almost 9 for about 200 percent profit. It would then have been rebought in late 1977 at about 6½ and sold in early 1980 at about 9½.

CASE HISTORY: *Using trend lines and channels to buy and sell stock in Fab Industries*

We have already discussed the performance of this company's stock vis-a-vis the Index of Merit. We can look at and directly compare what the shorter-term trader would have done with exactly the same data. The short-term trader would have bought this stock at about 1 in December 1974 and January 1975 strictly on the basis that it was an absolute steal; book value of $5.63, earnings of 27¢ per share, depreciation of 50¢ per share, for a total cash flow of 77¢ per share and selling for $1.

Watch Figure 8.7. An upper trend line was quickly established in early 1975. A line parallel to this line through the average of the lows could also have been drawn to give a lower limit line. This lower limit line was broken, however, in Au-

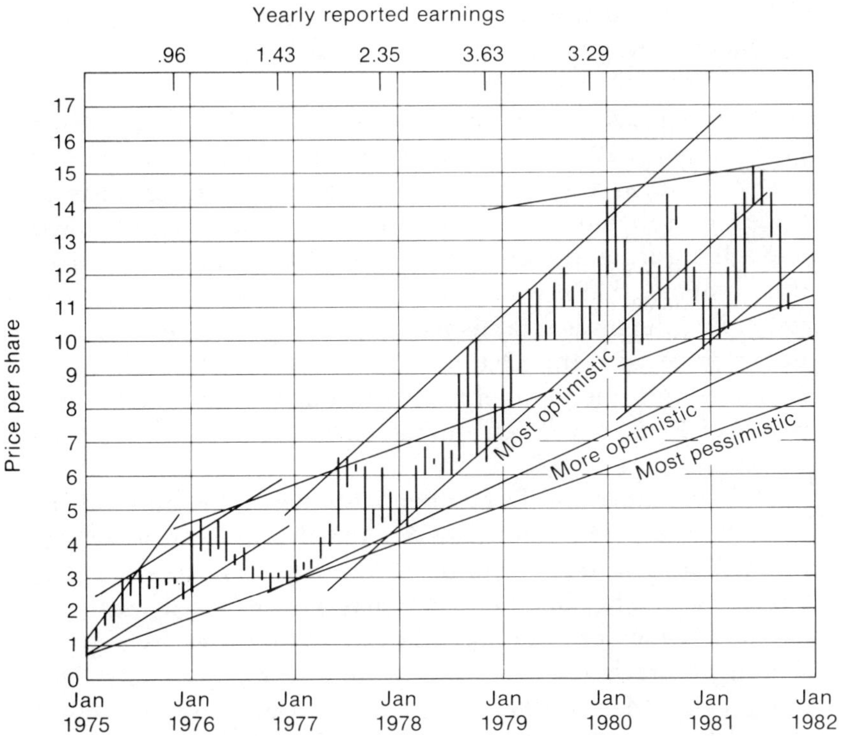

FIGURE 8.7. Performance of Fab Industries stock and its trend lines

gust 1975 and a more reliable lower limit established in February 1976. A new upper limit line was drawn parallel to this line through the peaks of May 1975 and January 1976. At least partial selling was indicated in February and April 1976, and buying should have started again in June and continued through March 1977. The performance data would have established a new lower trend line connecting the low of January 1975 and the lows of the latter part of 1976. An upper trend line was drawn parallel to this line through the high of February 1976. In June 1977 the upper limit line was reached and all shares were sold.

It was March 1978 before there were any clues that maybe

the lower trend line was too pessimistic. The lowest more optimistic line was drawn and some tentative buying of the stock commenced at about 5¼. In August, stock should have been sold at the upper trend line at about 7½. Actually, the price went to 10 in September but then the October 1978 massacre hit, and the price dropped to 6½. For the short-term trader in Fab stock, the October 1978 massacre supplied enough information on the performance characteristics of this company that it was almost like a license to steal. A new upper limit line was established connecting the June–July 1977 upper price with the October–November 1978 upper price. A lower limit line parallel to this through all the lower limit points of 1978 actually encompassed all the data back to June 1976.

In November and December 1978 there were all kinds of opportunities to buy between 6½ and 7½. In January 1979 it was still a good buy up to 8. At 11, in March, it was SELL, SELL, SELL. The October 1979 massacre brought the price down to the lower limit and a buy at 10, followed by a quick sellout in late January at 13½ in time to miss the late February–early March 1980 massacre. In March, reinvestment should have started at about 10 and continued as the price dropped to 8. The violation of the lower limit line should have tempered the timing and quantity of shares purchased.

Interestingly, the 1980 massacre eventually brought the price of this stock almost to the lower limit line that was drawn in March 1978. This was an indication that this stock might be starting a reversal. Therefore, when the stock reached 14 in August 1980, profits should have been taken even though the price was not up to the major upper trend line. In February 1981 a new trend line was drawn between the March 1980 low and the lows of December 1980. Purchases during the first three months of 1981 at prices between 10 and 11 were justified. In July 1981 an upper trend line was drawn between the February 1980 and the June 1981 tops. Note this line is not parallel to the lower trend line. This is an indication of a topping out of this stock, so sales at 14 in August were justified.

CASE HISTORY: Using trend lines and channels to buy and sell stock in Borden, Inc.

This company trades on the NYSE. During the early months of 1974, this stock dropped in price along with almost everything else. It hit bottom, however, in the middle of 1974, whereas most stocks hit bottom in December. Actually, there was no good reason for it to drop at all as earnings continued to increase throughout 1974 just as they had been doing for many years. By October 1975 a channel had formed which lasted through most of 1977. This stock continued to perform well in comparison to the remainder of the market in 1977.

From Figure 8.8 it is apparent that several profitable trades could have been made in this period.

Buy October 1975 at 23	Sell January 1976 at 29½	28 percent profit
Buy May 1976 at 26½	Sell August 1976 at 33	25 percent profit

In September 1977, purchases at 32 were indicated at the lower trend line. In November 1977, however, the price broke decisively on the down side and even though earnings were expected to increase, this stock should have been sold at about 31. A clear down channel was apparent in May 1978. To say the least, this downward trend was not justified; 1978 earnings would be $4.38 per share, and increasing, and the dividend was reasonable. Therefore this stock should have been watched closely as a possible buy. This downtrend continued until the early part of 1980. In June 1980 this stock broke out on the up side and a lower trend line was drawn in January 1981.

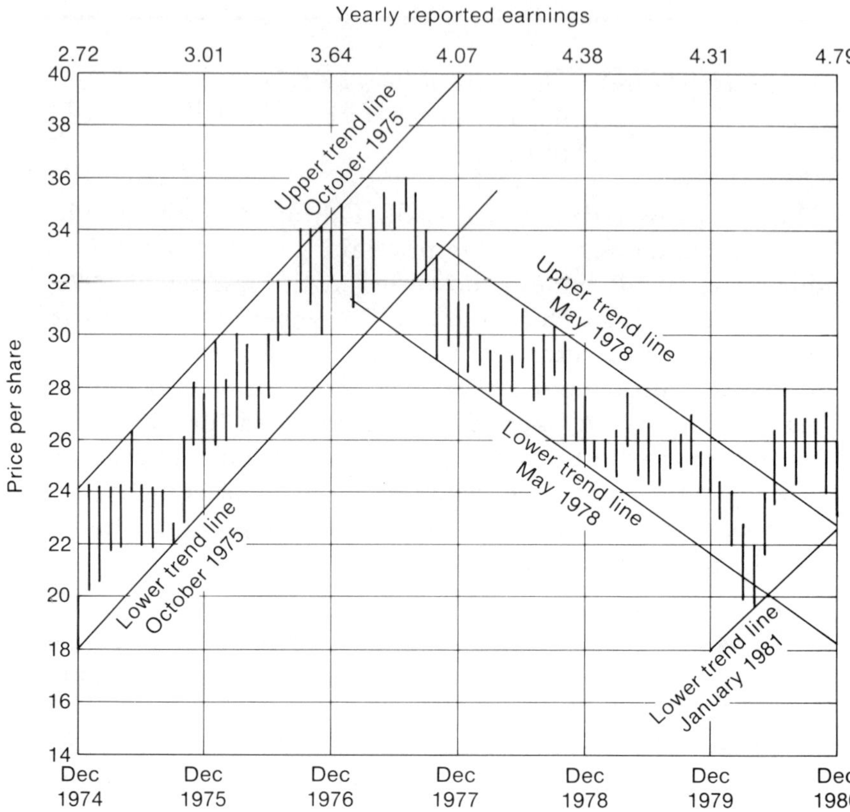

FIGURE 8.8. Performance of Borden Inc. stock and its trend lines

Using the Index of Merit and trend lines are two simple methods for determining when to make your stock transactions. The next chapter will summarize how to make this total system work as you manage your portfolio of stocks.

Your Action Steps

- Calculate the Index of Merit and the buy point for the past two years, if you have the time, or for the past two quarters at least, on the back of the S&P or Moody's sheet for each of the stocks in your reservoir.

- Plot the Index of Merit and the buy point on a chart for each stock in your reservoir.
- If you wish, draw trend lines on your S&P or Moody's charts.
- Calculate a new Index of Merit and buy point each time a new earnings report comes out for any of your stocks.

Chapter 9

MANAGING YOUR PORTFOLIO

Finally, we get to the heart of the system—your portfolio, those stocks you own. You will want to collect certain weekly information on these stocks as well as longer-term information for your tax records. This chapter discusses

- how the whole system fits together
- daily, weekly, and quarterly activities you'll need to undertake to make the system work
- how to make objective buying and selling decisions based on the data you've collected and interpreted

Collecting Data on Your Portfolio

Start by labelling another divider tab in your binder "Portfolio." Rule off seventeen columns on the first sheet of binder paper following the divider and label the columns as shown in Figure 9.1. This will be used for your weekly summary of the action of the stocks you own.

You should list your Amex stocks first in alphabetical order, and then your NYSE stocks in alphabetical order. You can obtain the Friday closing price for each from your broker on Friday afternoon or from many papers on Saturday morning; on the West Coast some papers have this data in the Friday evening paper. Calculate the change for the week from the previous week's data sheet and mark it either + or –.

The fifth, seventh, and ninth columns can be copied from last week's sheet, corrected, of course, for any changes that

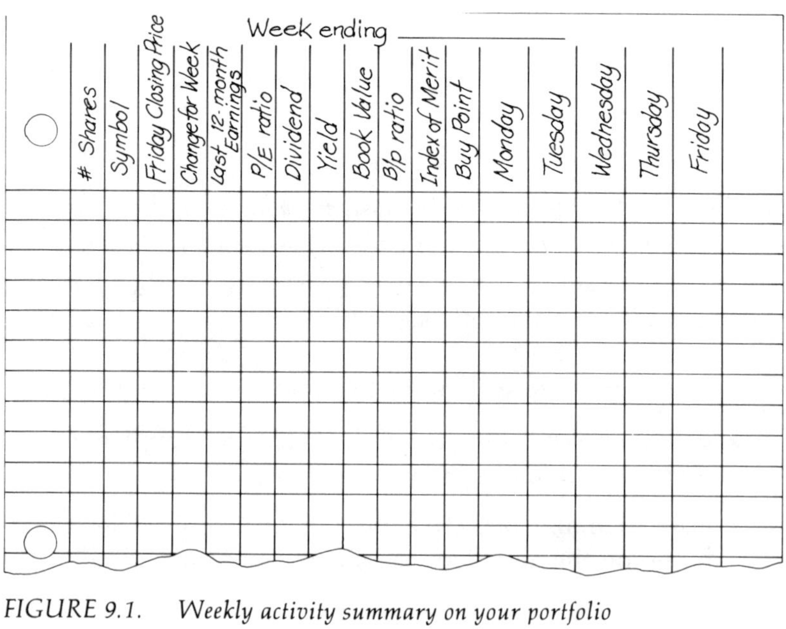

FIGURE 9.1. Weekly activity summary on your portfolio

may have occurred in the past week. The sixth, eighth, and tenth columns are calculated with your calculator as follows:

- P/E ratio = Friday closing price ÷ last twelve months' earnings
- Yield = annual dividend ÷ Friday closing price
- B/P ratio = book value ÷ Friday closing price

The eleventh and twelfth columns are labelled Index of Merit and Buy Point respectively. These figures can be transferred directly from last week's sheet unless a new earnings report has been issued in the past week. The last five columns are for recording the daily close of your stocks in the coming week.

To better visualize the performance of your portfolio this past week, it is helpful to write a positive change in green and a negative change in red. Circle in green all the P/E ratios that are less than 5.0, all the yields that are greater than 6.5 percent, and all the B/P ratios greater than 1.5. If a stock has all three items circled, it is a prime candidate for additional buying. If a stock has none of these items circled, it is a prime candidate for selling. If you have a particularly attractive stock in mind to buy, but must first sell something from your portfolio, this is where to look first. Table 9.1 is an example of the way your weekly table will look when it is set up.

In addition to the weekly data on your portfolio, you will want to keep a record of your transactions. Set up a separate sheet for each stock. Rule off six columns and head them as shown in Table 9.2. You will note that this order of the data is the same as required by income tax form 1040D so it will make things easier for you at tax time. After the profit or loss, add the code LT for a long-term or ST for a short-term profit or loss, as defined by the Internal Revenue Service.

Finally, you might want to start several tally sheets to make things easy at tax time:

- long-term gains
- short-term gains

TABLE 9.1. Completed Weekly Portfolio Data

# SHARES	SYMBOL	FRIDAY CLOSING	CHANGE FOR WEEK	LAST 12 MONTHS' EARNINGS	P/E RATIO	DIVIDEND	YIELD	BOOK VALUE	B/P RATIO	INDEX OF MERIT	BUY POINT
400	CWK	7	+⅜	1.07	6.54	.60	8.57	9.36	1.34	7.5	5.3
1600	CRW	4⅞	+⅛	.70	6.90	.20	4.10	10.00	2.05	6.5	4.6
1350	FIT	11⅛	+¼	2.84	3.92	.50	4.49	11.01	.99	12.7	8.9
	• • •										
200	WLC	4⅛	−⅜	.29	14.22	.25	6.06	12.57	3.05	7.2	5.0
200	BNY	12	+¼	2.33	5.14	.88	7.33	15.55	1.30	15.0	10.5
	• • •										
800	VX	14⅜	+1⅝	2.58	5.57	.68	4.73	16.05	1.12	16.2	11.3

- dividends received
- interest received
- interest paid if you have a margin account

At the time you record a stock sale as shown in Table 9.2, also record the same data in the same order on either the long- or short-term tally sheet as appropriate. When you receive your monthly statement from your broker, add all dividends shown on that statement to your dividend tally sheet; enter the amount of the dividend beside the stock name. If you have any bonds, record the amount received on your tally sheet when you receive the information on your monthly statement. Likewise, if you have a margin account, record the amount of interest paid each month on a tally sheet when you receive your monthly statement.

TABLE 9.2. *Completed Stock Transaction Table*

		CHADWICK MILLER (CWK) AMERICAN			
QUANTITY	PURCHASE DATE	SALE DATE	SALE PRICE	PURCHASE PRICE	PROFIT
100	12/20/74	2/14/76	550	325	+ 225 LT
100	2/10/75	2/14/76	535	420	+ 115 LT
100	8/14/75	2/15/76	550	375	+ 75 ST
200	8/8/76	2/14/78	1600	950	+ 650 LT
400	10/7/76	2/14/78	3200	2000	+1200 LT
400	10/27/78			2400	
100	11/5/78	1/9/81	950	650	+ 300 LT
100	11/12/78			650	

TABLE 9.3. Long-term (1976) Gains Tally Sheet

		PURCHASES		SALES		PROFIT
QUANTITY	NAME	DATE	PRICE	DATE	PRICE	
100	Chadwick-Miller	12/20/74	325	2/14/76	550	+225
100	Chadwick-Miller	2/10/75	420	2/14/76	535	+115
200	Crown Crafts	3/11/75	310	4/15/76	1100	+790
100	Blessings	12/12/74	450	4/19/76	575	+125
100	Buildex	1/10/75	420	5/10/76	350	-70

TABLE 9.4. *Dividends Received Tally Sheet*

SHARES	COMPANY	ANNUAL RATE	RECEIVED				TOTAL
500	Blessings	.66	82.50	82.50			
100	IBM	3.44	86.00	86.00			
400	Jaclyn	.40 + stock	40.00	16 shares 40.00			
.							
.							
.							
100	Borden	2.06	51.50				

Keeping Track of Net Worth

It is very important to be aware of your net worth on a continuing basis. Is it increasing or decreasing? How rapidly? You should also set at least annual and probably even final goals for net worth. Most people understate their net worth; they forget such things as the cash value of insurance policies, the value of household goods, appreciation of a home, etc. The following is one possible way to break down net worth:

- net value of stock account
- net value of bond account
- net value of IRAs and Keoghs
- cash, savings accounts, cash value of insurance policies
- net value of home
- value of other property, such as auto, furniture, etc.

After you receive your monthly statement from your broker, you can plot your net worth as shown in Figure 9.2.

If the price of real estate is going up, you should determine the approximate rate of increase, and increase the value assigned to your home by that amount each month. There is a minor problem when one purchases, for cash, a capital item such as a new refrigerator or a new car. Actually, your net worth has not decreased by this purchase so at the end of the month the purchase price of the refrigerator or car must be added to the value of your household goods in the month of purchase. In the following month, however, if no capital goods are purchased, the value of household goods should be depreciated to account for the depreciation of major items such as TV, automobile, appliances, etc. Taxes are accounted for quarterly as they are paid and, of course, they show up as a decrease in net worth either in your cash account or in one of your stock market accounts, if stock is sold to pay taxes.

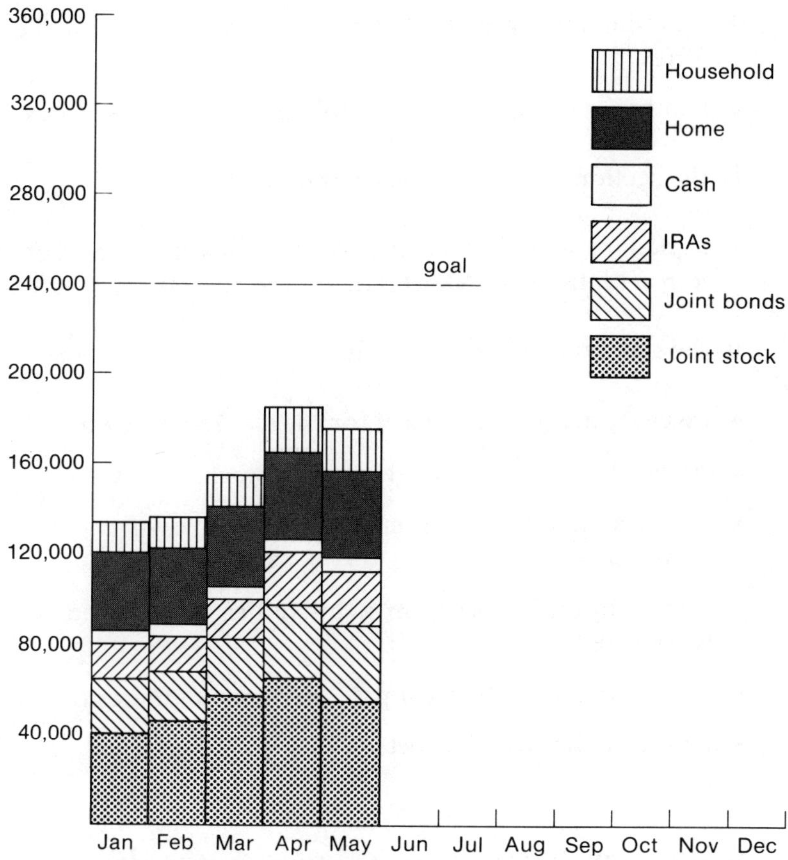

FIGURE 9.2. Monthly plot of net worth

Summary: The Elements of the System

Your binder encompassing the system is now complete. Let us review the elements it should contain.

In the section labelled "Market Averages":

- a moving averages table for the NYSE and one for the Amex

- a moving averages chart for the NYSE and one for the Amex
- a daily pulse chart for the NYSE and one for the Amex

In the section labelled "Reservoir of stocks:"

- an S&P or Moody's sheet for each stock in your reservoir, with Index of Merit data on the reverse side

In the section labelled "Portfolio":

- a weekly activity summary for the stocks you own
- the S&P or Moody's sheet for each stock you own
- a transaction table for each stock you own or have owned this year
- long-term and short-term gains tallies as required for 1040D tax form
- tallies for margin interest paid, dividends, interest
- a monthly net worth chart

Summary: Periodic Activity Required of You

Assuming that you have set your system up as described and have up-to-date and historical data available on S&P or Moody's sheets, the following periodic activity will be required of you to keep the system running.

Each evening you will need to. . .

- obtain daily market data (volume traded, number of issues advancing, number of issues declining, close of the market average) on both the NYSE and the Amex from your broker or the *Wall Street Journal*
- plot the data on your daily pulse charts

- draw or revise trend lines on the daily pulse charts if appropriate
- scan the earnings digest and dividend section of the *Wall Street Journal* for new data on any of the stocks in your reservoir; enter new data onto the S&P or Moody's sheet and recalculate Index of Merit and buy point
- record daily close prices of stocks in your portfolio

Each weekend, you will need to. . .

- obtain from the Saturday or Sunday paper the Friday close of the two market averages; enter the data on the proper moving averages table and calculate the current moving averages; plot this data on the moving averages chart for each exchange
- study the moving averages chart for each exchange and mark buy or sell signals if they are present
- draw or revise trend lines if appropriate on the moving averages charts
- obtain from the Saturday or Sunday paper the weekly close, the price range, and the volume traded for each of the stocks in your reservoir, and tabulate on your S&P or Moody's sheets; draw or revise trend lines on your S&P or Moody's charts.
- obtain from the Saturday or Sunday paper the Friday close for each of the stocks in your portfolio; enter the data on the S&P or Moody's sheets as above, and in addition, enter the Friday close into the weekly activity summary and calculate the change for the week and the new P/E ratio, yield, and B/P ratio, and prepare the activity summary sheet for next week.

Quarterly you will need to. . .

- recalculate the Index of Merit and the buy point for

individual stocks as new earnings reports come out or dividends are declared (this will be at different times for different stocks, although at quarterly intervals for each)

As you make stock purchases or sales, you will need to. . .

- record your transaction on the transaction record for the individual stock
- record the profit or loss on the long-term or short-term gains tally sheet required for 1040D

Summary: Instructions for Buying and Selling

Now that you have a collection of sound data on which to base your buying and selling decisions, all you need is a simple, clear set of instructions for acting on that data. Here it is.

Watch your moving averages charts.

- If a *bear market is in progress,* don't buy anything.
- At the *first buy signal,* use about 20 percent of your capital to buy at least five stocks that are priced below their buy points. The stocks selected should be the most underpriced stocks in your reservoir.
- At the *second buy signal,* use about 30 percent of your capital to buy at least five additional stocks that are priced below their buy points.
- At the *third and final buy signal,* invest the remainder of your funds in stocks that are priced at or near their buy points. Some of these might be stocks that you have purchased on previous buy signals.

- As the *bull market progresses,* start selling stocks as their prices approach their Index of Merit or upper trend line.
- As the moving averages *stay in a bull market configuration,* buy additional shares of stocks whose prices are at the buy point to replace shares sold.
- As the *bull market progresses,* buy shares of stock at prices slightly above their buy points if they are near their historical low prices or historical low P/E ratios.
- Watch the trend lines of your market averages. As the *market average rises to the upper trend line,* sell about 20 percent of your portfolio; at least 20 percent of your stocks will be at their upper trend line or Index of Merit when this occurs.
- Watch the daily pulse of the market. As *trend lines, volume, and/or advancing/declining issues are unfavorable,* start some precautionary selling.
- At the *first sell signal,* sell about 20 percent of your portfolio.
- At the *second sell signal,* sell about 30 percent of your portfolio.
- At the *third and final sell signal,* sell the remainder of your portfolio and wait for the next bull market.

Part IV

RELATED INVESTMENT CONSIDERATIONS

Chapter 10

U.S. TREASURY BONDS AND NOTES

For many years, the bond market and particularly the treasury bond market was a quiet, sleepy place for the most part. The price of U.S. Treasury bonds moved a percentage point or two over a period of months. They were the ideal investment for retired persons who wanted an assured fixed income with no risk to capital. Industrial bonds were slightly more risky but generally paid a higher return. Since 1979, however, things have changed; bond prices now seem to swell and ebb over a wide range like stock prices. Therefore, bonds can be bought and sold in the same way as stocks are. All the techniques described for trading stocks can be applied to trading bonds. In this chapter we will look at

- the performance of bonds in the recent past
- some strategies for making money with bonds

Long-Term U.S. Treasury Bonds and Notes

Figure 10.1 is a plot of the weekly closing price of the February 2000 U.S. Treasury bond paying 7⅞ percent interest per year. The price quoted is per $100 worth of bond. Of course, these bonds are not available in $100 denominations; with treasury bonds, $100,000 worth is a round lot. When this bond was originally issued, it sold for about $1000 and the going interest rate on bonds of this maturity length was about 8 percent.

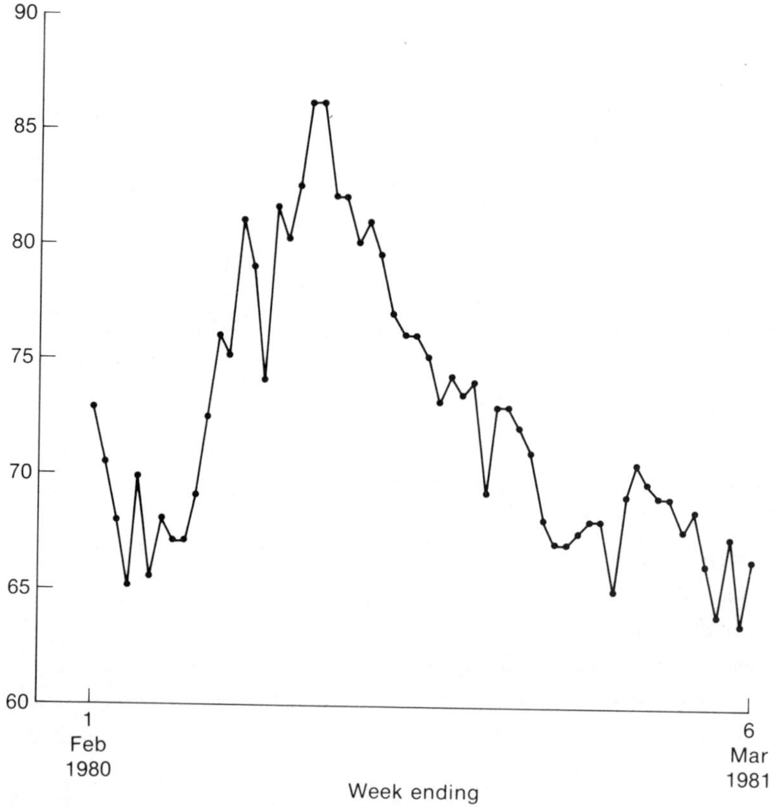

FIGURE 10.1. *The weekly closing price of the February 2000 U.S. Treasury bond at 7⅞ percent interest, Feb. 1980–Mar. 1981*

Because of high interest rates and the threat of continued inflation, the price of the bond had decreased to $65 in March 1981 so that the effective yield was comparable to that of a bond that was issued in March 1981 at $1000 with the same maturity date. If you had bought this bond in March 1981, the yield would have been about 12 percent and in addition you will have a capital gain of about $330 per $1000 bond in the year 2000.

Long-term bonds available at low prices offer many opportunities for making money. Retirees and others who already own a portfolio of bonds bought at high prices can enhance their net worth with a simple transaction.

Suppose, for example, that a person retired several years ago and bought $100,000 face value of the February 2000 bonds when they were issued and paid $100,000. Yearly interest on these bonds is $7875. The retiree in March 1981 could have sold these bonds for $67,000 and bought for $67,000 a different bond with a face value of $100,000 paying 12 percent, which is $8000 per year. After these transactions, the retiree would have had exactly the same value of bonds and approximately the same interest per year as before. But in addition, the investor would have had a $33,000 tax loss, to apply against 1981 capital gains and $3000 worth of ordinary interest income. Likewise, any unused part of this loss could have been carried over to subsequent years to offset capital gains and ordinary income.

Buying on margin is usually not advisable for a retiree on a fixed income. Bonds, however, offer a unique opportunity to obtain large capital gains at minimum cost and risk. Suppose our investor retired in early 1980 with $65,000 to invest in bonds. The absolutely safe strategy would be to purchase $100,000 face value of February 2000 bonds and to collect their return of $7875 each year to maturity. An alternative strategy would be to purchase $200,000 face value of these bonds for $130,000. Of course, this strategy can only be profitable if there is a high probability that bond prices are low at the time of purchase, which was certainly true in March 1980. To make this purchase our retiree could have put up his or her

$65,000 for half the bonds and borrowed $65,000 from a broker for the other half. On the bonds bought with the borrowed money, the retiree would have paid interest at a rate of about 20 percent per year. But this interest cost would have been offset by the 12 percent interest received on the bond, so the effective interest cost would have been only 8 percent per annum or .67 percent per month on $65,000. By June, the price of these bonds had increased to over $85 each.

Let us assume that our investor missed the exact top but sold $100,000 face amount of these bonds at $80 in July. The total cost of the investment would have been $65,000 × .67 percent interest × five months, or approximately $2200. Total return would have been $80,000 – $65,000, or $15,000, for a $12,800 profit. The return on this investment would have been almost 600 percent for only five months. Actually the total profit would have been greater than calculated because the cost of the investment (net interest paid) is tax deductible. It should also be noted that our investor would still have received the interest throughout this period from his $65,000 investment and would still own $100,000 face amount of these bonds; he would just be $13,000 richer.

Of course, the investor would have been taking some risk with the above strategy. The price of the bonds could have decreased during the period. This is not likely if they are bought based on ten-, fifteen-, and twenty-week moving averages. If it should happen, however, repeat the procedure from some lower base price; sell, for example, $100,000 worth of your present bonds and buy $100,000 worth of a different bond.

Monitoring the Bond Market

Prior to 1980, it didn't make much sense to monitor the bond market because the changes were so slight and gradual. You must monitor the present bond market if you intend to invest in bonds for capital gains or are planning to purchase a bond portfolio for impending retirement and a steady income. There are dozens of different U.S. Treasury bonds and notes from which you can choose. These bonds and notes have different maturity dates and different interest rates. However, they all move in unison so only one long- and one medium-term bond must be monitored to be representative of all long-

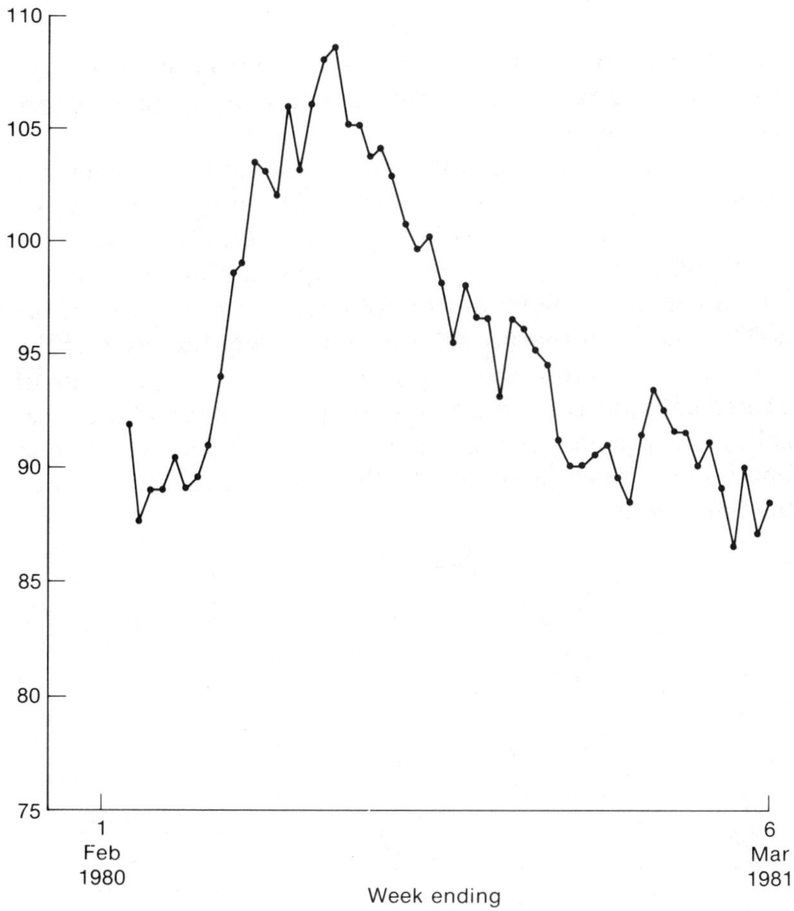

FIGURE 10.2. *The weekly closing price of the November 1989 U.S. Treasury note at 10¾ percent interest, Feb. 1980–Mar. 1981*

and medium-term bonds. To be more precise, however, it is recommended that you also plot the movement of a short-term bond. You should plot the movement of the following three issues:

- February 2000, 7⅞ percent
- November 1990, 13 percent
- November 1985, 11¾ percent

You should calculate the ten-, fifteen-, and twenty-week moving averages and use the same rules to monitor them as are used with stocks on the NYSE.

Figure 10.2 is a plot of the weekly close of the November 1989, 10¾ U.S. Treasury note. An interesting fact is noted when this figure is compared to Figure 10.1. From the February 1980 low to the June 1980 high, the amount of the increase is exactly the same for both. However, the price of the 2000 bond in February was much lower than the price of the 1989 note. Therefore, the long-term bond had a capital gain of 31 percent whereas the intermediate-term note had a capital gain of only 23 percent. The percent increase and decrease in bonds and notes is larger, the further out the maturity dates of the bond or note.

Chapter 11
INVESTING FOR RETIREMENT

This chapter is written for the investor who has been successful and accumulated a reasonable net worth and who is presently employed but facing either forced or desired retirement in only a few years. Such an investor is faced with the questions, "Can I afford to retire at sixty?" or "What will my standard of living be like if I am forced to retire at sixty-five?" Regardless of your net worth, you will need to precalculate what would happen under a variety of different scenarios. Then if everything calculates out okay for retirement next week, you can go ahead and retire. More than likely, however, problems will be apparent and then it will be necessary to make plans so that you can retire at some specific date in the future. The purpose of this chapter is to help you

- think about the future in an informed way
- plan to modify your portfolio prior to or at retirement

Calculate Basic Information

Most of the data needed for a good financial analysis of potential retirement income are readily available at any point in time. Most of your present data will be quite reliable and you can reasonably estimate changes in the data. The biggest uncertainty is how long you (and your spouse) will live. All other uncertainties such as the inflation rate and the performance of the stock and bond markets can be estimated pessimistically or optimistically, as you wish.

Prepare a Budget. The first step in determining whether you can afford to retire now is to prepare a budget for right now. What do you spend or what have you spent in the last year on fundamentals?

- food
- housing
- clothing
- operation of auto
- operation of household
- utilities
- medical expenses
- miscellaneous (insurance, etc.)

Note that this budget does not include the purchase of capital goods such as furniture or cars, recreation or travel. This is a bare-bones budget; only the necessities of life. Now let us assume that inflation will be 10 percent a year compounded annually over the remainder of your life. You can compute your projected annual budgets with a hand calculator in less than ten minutes.

Enter and store in memory your first budget. Multiply by 0.1 and add the product to memory. Recall from memory what is now next year's budget. Multiply this by 0.1 and add the product to memory; recall from memory what is now the second year's budget. Continue until you have about twenty annual budgets.

Tabulate Your Assets and Income Now and in the Future. To simplify matters we will assume that you have a home that is paid for, and therefore your only housing expenses will be taxes and maintenance. Such a home is an asset that will probably appreciate, and, if necessary, can be sold at a later date to obtain capital for investment to generate additional income. We will assume that such is not the case.

Your first source of income will be your retirement pay. In some cases this will be a fixed sum; if it is $10,000 now, it will be $10,000 per year ten years from now. Many companies do regularly increase pension payments voluntarily while other employers such as the government must increase payments by law. Let us assume that you will retire from a company which has raised pensions periodically on a voluntary basis and will continue to do so. The only question is how much of an increase should you expect. You should be conservative in this expectation; if you used 10 percent for inflation, use about 4 percent here. Find out what your retirement pay will be if you retire today or next year or at any other proposed date. Start with this number and using the same procedure as described for the budget, calculate your expected pension income for each year over the next twenty years.

Your second source of income will be your Social Security pay. You can easily obtain from the Social Security Administration an estimate of what your benefits will be for a given retirement date. Again, this retirement benefit is tied to the cost of living. Therefore, you must take the initial sum to be received annually and calculate the expected sum to be received annually for future years. This calculation is made in the same way as your budget. Again, to be conservative you should use about 4 percent and calculate for about twenty years.

Your third source of income will be dividends from stocks. It is a good idea to have a portion of your retirement capital in stocks that have a high dividend and a record of frequent dividend increases. The price of the stocks will increase with the years as the dividend increases. The dividends you expect to receive on your retirement date must be incremented each year over the next twenty years by about 4 percent each year using the procedure previously described.

Your fourth source of income should be capital gains. About 25 percent of your capital should be in stocks that were bought in the safe buy zones described in Chapter 8. You should expect about 20 percent return per year on these investments. This income is not compounded. It is expected that you will spend the profit but the capital will remain invested.

Your final source of income will be interest from relatively long-term bonds. As discussed in Chapter 10, for most investors and retirees in particular, U.S. Treasury bonds or notes will give the greatest peace of mind. However, after you have calculated your situation, you might find that you have to give up some security to obtain higher yield from utilities or industrial bonds.

If you retire early, you may expect to have some earnings from odd jobs, consulting, etc. after retirement. This should be included under other income, if it is a reasonably assured source of income.

CASE HISTORY: *Retirement at age sixty*

Let's look at an individual age fifty-nine with a salary of $40,000 per year, a budget of $13,000 per year for this year, a portfolio of stocks worth $100,000 paying $5000 in dividends per year, company retirement of $7000 per year at age sixty, and Social Security payments starting at age sixty-five of $7000 per year. Can this individual afford to retire next year? Using the procedures described above, Table 11.1 is constructed.

TABLE 11.1. Retirement Balance Sheet, 1982–89

INCOME	1982	1983	1984	1985	1986	1987	1988	1989
Salary	$40,000	—	—	—	—	—	—	—
Retirement	—	$7000	$7280	$7571	$7874	$8189	$8517	$8856
Social Security	—	—	—	—	—	—	$7000	$7280
Dividends	$5000	$5200	$5408	$5624	$5849	$6083	$6327	$6580
Total Income	$45,000	$12,000	$12,688	$13,195	$13,723	$14,272	$21,844	$22,716
EXPENSES								
Budget	$13,000	$14,300	$15,730	$17,303	$19,033	$20,937	$23,030	$25,333
Taxes	$9000	$2000	$2000	$2000	$2000	$2000	$2000	$2000
Total	$22,000	$16,300	$17,730	$19,303	$21,033	$22,937	$25,030	$27,333
Savings and/or extras in living	$23,000	-$4100	-$5042	-$6108	-$7310	-$8665	-$3186	-$4617

This individual is in trouble if he or she retires next year at sixty. If an absolute bare budget is maintained this year, the $23,000 in savings will just cover the deficits through 1986 provided those years are also bare-budget years. But from 1987 on, deficits will have to be met from capital, which will shortly thereafter be exhausted. The deficits in the years before drawing Social Security could be erased by part-time work for about $5000 per year after retirement, but this would only delay the problem, not correct it.

Let us look at some rearrangements of assets as a solution to the problem, and let's suppose that the individual can reasonably expect to earn about $4000 per year during the years up to age sixty-five. Suppose that his or her present portfolio of stocks contains $25,000 worth that are paying 8 percent, and that $25,000 worth have good potential for capital gains over the near term. If the potential retiree keeps the above stocks but sells the remaining $50,000 worth of stocks and buys U.S. Treasury bonds paying, say, 12 percent, Table 11.2 shows what will happen out to 1989.

This is certainly a better picture than the initial one. The picture can be even better if we assume that our retiree saves, for example, $20,000 of the 1982 excess income and invests it in bonds. There are some uncertainties and negative elements in this picture: capital gains of 20 percent, other income of $4000 per year, and the average excess of about $3000 per year must cover all capital expenses such as cars and refrigerators that must be replaced and all travel and recreational expenses. By 1991, this excess will be negative which means that survival will require going into capital, which will have the added detrimental effect of decreasing income. Table 11.3 shows what will happen through 1998. Note the bonds have been broken down into five different maturity dates for clarity.

Obviously our retiree is again in trouble but starting in 1991. If we assume that our retiree saved about $20,000 of 1982 salary and invested this money in bonds at, say, 12 percent, then the income from these bonds could cover the deficits in the years from 1991 to 1996. But these would have to be sold along with some stock to make up the deficit of

TABLE 11.2 Revised Retirement Balance Sheet, 1982–89

INCOME	1982	1983	1984	1985	1986	1987	1988	1989
Salary	$40,000							
Retirement	—	$7000	$7280	$7571	$7874	$8189	$8517	$8856
Social Security	—	—	—	—	—	—	$7000	$7280
($25,000) Dividends 8%	$2000	$2080	$2163	$2250	$2340	$2433	$2531	$2632
($50,000) Bond Int. 12%	$6000	$6000	$6000	$6000	$6000	$6000	$6000	$6000
($25,000) Capital Gains (20%)	$5000	$5000	$5000	$5000	$5000	$5000	$5000	$5000
Other Income	—	$4000	$4000	$4000	$4000	$4000	—	—
Total	$53,000	$24,080	$24,443	$24,821	$25,214	$25,622	$29,048	$29,768
EXPENSES								
Budget	$13,000	$14,300	$15,730	$17,303	$19,033	$20,937	$23,030	$25,333
Taxes	$9000	$4000	$4000	$4000	$4000	$4000	$2000	$2000
Total	$22,000	$18,300	$19,730	$21,303	$23,033	$24,937	$25,030	$27,333
Savings and/or extras in living	$31,000	$5780	$4713	$3518	$2181	$683	$4018	$2435

TABLE 11.3. Retirement Balance Sheet, 1990–98

INCOME	1990	1991	1992	1993	1994	1995	1996	1997	1998
Retirement	$9210	$9579	$9962	$10,360	$10,775	$11,206	$11,654	$12,120	$12,605
Social Security	$7571	$7874	$8189	$8517	$8857	$9212	$9580	$9963	$10,362
($25,000) Dividend Stocks–8%	$2737	$2848	$2961	$3079	$3202	$3330	$3464	$3602	$3746
($10,000) Bonds–12%	$1200	$1200	$1200	$10,000*	—	—	—	—	—
($10,000) Bonds–12%	$1200	$1200	$1200	$1200	$10,000*	—	—	—	—
($10,000) Bonds–12%	$1200	$1200	$1200	$1200	$1200	$10,000*	—	—	—
($10,000) Bonds–12%	$1200	$1200	$1200	$1200	$1200	$1200	$10,000*	—	—
($10,000) Bonds–12%	$1200	$1200	$1200	$1200	$1200	$1200	$10,000*	—	—
($25,000) Capital Gain Stocks–(20%)	$5000	$5000	$5000	$5000	$5000	$5000	$5000	$25,000*	—
Total	$30,518	$31,301	$32,112	$41,756	$41,434	$41,148	$49,698	$50,685	$26,713
EXPENSES									
Budget	$27,866	$30,653	$33,718	$37,090	$40,799	$44,879	$49,367	$54,304	$59,734
Taxes	$2000	$2000	$2000	$2000	$2000	$2000	$2000	$2000	$2000
Total	$29,866	$32,653	$35,718	$39,090	$42,799	$46,879	$51,367	$56,304	$61,734
Savings and/or extras for living	+$652	-$1352	-$3606	+$2666	-$1365	-$5731	-$1669	-$5619	-$35,021

*proceeds from bonds cashed

1998. With this plan, our retiree can retire at age sixty provided he or she is willing to live on a bare subsistence level and is sure to die before 1998 at the age of seventy-five.

The potential retiree should now recalculate his or her retirement income assuming an additional two or three years of work, saving as much as possible, and investing these savings for capital gains. The objective of the program should be to accumulate additional capital prior to retirement so that the income needs of each retirement year are satisfied. Assume that $75,000 is invested in stocks that have a potential for 20 percent capital gains per year while the investor continues to work, and that $50,000 of this will be converted on retirement to bonds paying 10 percent. It should be noted that the bonds should be purchased with maturity dates in years that you identify as ones when you will be needing funds.

Table 11.4 shows our retiree's plan with an additional two years of work. Through 1989 everything is fine for our retiree. He or she is keeping the same basic standard of living as at retirement and there is an average annual excess of better than $6000 for recreation and travel or purchase of capital items. Note that for this case we presume that when the bonds are purchased only a 10 percent return is available. This might be conservative. Likewise, we have assumed the worst case on inflation and also the worst case on increases in Social Security and pension. In 1992 the first sign of a problem appears. It will be necessary to sell a $10,000 bond to prevent a deficit. The proceeds from this sale will be spread over 1992 and 1993 and will maintain a positive surplus (but only about $3000 average) for the 1990 to 1993 period. Bonds will have to be sold as indicated through 1994 to 1997 to obtain an average excess of only $1000.

Even with sales of all remaining bonds and stocks, our retiree will be reduced to zero capital by 2000. By this time our retiree will be seventy-seven years old. This is still not an absolutely safe plan, but considering that our retiree has had a reasonable excess of cash over the bare necessities and considering that all calculations are on worst case, it is probably reasonable. A little more savings in the last working years and

TABLE 11.4 A Second Possible Retirement Balance Sheet, 1982–2000

INCOME	1982	1983	1984	1985
Salary	$40,000	$40,000	$40,000	–
Retirement	–	–	–	$7500
Social Security	–	–	–	–
($25,000) Dividend Stocks–8%	$2000	$2080	$2163	$2250
($75,000) Capital Gain Stocks–20%	$15,000	$15,000	$15,000	$5000
($10,000) Bond–10%	–	–	–	$1000
($10,000) Bond–10%	–	–	–	$1000
($10,000) Bond–10%	–	–	–	$1000
($10,000) Bond–10%	–	–	–	$1000
($10,000) Bond–10%	–	–	–	$1000
(a) ($20,000) Bond–10%	–	$2000	$2000	$2000
(b) ($20,000) Bond–10%	–	–	$2000	$2000
(c) ($20,000) Bond–10%	–	–	–	$2000
Other Income	–	–	–	$4000
Total	$57,000	$59,080	$61,163	$29,750
EXPENSES				
Budget	$13,000	$14,300	$15,730	$17,303
Taxes	$12,000	$12,000	$12,000	$5000
Total	$25,000	$26,300	$27,730	$22,303
Savings and/or extras for living	+$32,000 ↑ Buy bond (a) with part of excess	+$32,780 ↑ Buy bond (b) with part of excess	+$33,433 ↑ Buy bond (c) with part of excess	+$7447

TABLE 11.4. (cont.)

1986	1987	1988	1989	1990	1991
—	—	—	—	—	—
$7800	$8112	$8436	$8774	$9125	$9490
—	—	$7200	$7488	$7788	$8099
$2340	$2433	$2531	$2632	$2737	$2848
$5000	$5000	$5000	$5000	$5000	$5000
$1000	$1000	$1000	$1000	$1000	$1000
$1000	$1000	$1000	$1000	$1000	$1000
$1000	$1000	$1000	$1000	$1000	$1000
$1000	$1000	$1000	$1000	$1000	$1000
$1000	$1000	$1000	$1000	$1000	$1000
$2000	$2000	$2000	$2000	$2000	$2000
$2000	$2000	$2000	$2000	$2000	$2000
$2000	$2000	$2000	$2000	$2000	$2000
$4000	$4000	—	—	—	—
$30,140	$30,545	$34,167	$34,894	$35,650	$36,437
$19,033	$20,937	$23,030	$25,333	$27,866	$30,653
$5000	$5000	$3000	$3000	$3000	$3000
$24,033	$25,937	$26,030	$28,333	$30,866	$33,653
+$6107	+$4608	+$8137	+$6561	+$4784	+$2784

TABLE 11.4. (cont.)

INCOME	1992	1993	1994	1995
Salary	—	—	—	—
Retirement	$9870	$10,264	$10,675	$11,102
Social Security	$8423	$8760	$9110	$9475
($25,000) Dividend Stocks–8%	$2961	$3079	$3202	$3330
($75,000) Capital Gain Stocks–20%	$5000	$5000	$5000	$5000
($10,000) Bond–10%	$10,000*	—	—	—
($10,000) Bond–10%	$1000	$1000	$10,000*	—
($10,000) Bond–10%	$1000	$1000	$1000	$10,000*
($10,000) Bond–10%	$1000	$1000	$1000	$1000
($10,000) Bond–10%	$1000	$1000	$1000	$1000
(a) ($20,000) Bond–10%	$2000	$2000	$2000	$2000
(b) ($20,000) Bond–10%	$2000	$2000	$2000	$2000
(c) ($20,000) Bond–10%	$2000	$2000	$2000	$2000
Other Income	—	—	—	—
Total	$46,254	$37,103	$46,987	$46,907
EXPENSES				
Budget	$33,718	$37,090	$40,799	$44,879
Taxes	$3000	$3000	$3000	$3000
Total	$36,718	$40,090	$43,799	$47,879
Savings and/or extras for living	+$9536	–$2987	+$3188	–$972

* proceeds from bonds cashed
† proceeds from stock sold

1996	1997	1998	1999	2000
—	—	—	—	—
$11,546	$12,008	$12,488	$12,988	$13,507
$9854	$10,248	$10,658	$11,084	$11,527
$3464	$3602	$3746	$3896	$4052
$5000	$5000	$5000	$5000	$25,000†
—	—	—	—	—
—	—	—	—	—
—	—	—	—	—
$10,000*	—	—	—	—
$10,000*	—	—	—	—
$2000	$20,000*	—	—	—
$2000	$2000	$20,000*	—	—
$2000	$2000	$2000	$20,000*	—
—	—	—	—	—
$55,864	$54,858	$53,892	$52,968	$54,086
$49,367	$54,304	$59,734	$65,707	$72,278
$3000	$3000	$3000	$3000	$3000
$52,367	$57,304	$62,734	$68,707	$75,278
+$3497	–$2446	–$8842	–$15,739	–$21,192

a little more part-time work after retirement or a little more interest on the bonds would certainly extend the retirement income for several more years. This retiree should recalculate the plan with a slightly less conservative approach, for example with 9 percent inflation and 5 percent increments of Social Security and pension, and supplemental income of $6000 per year, with the additional funds being used to increase the capital gains stock portfolio.

It should be obvious that if our potential retiree at fifty-nine had about $200,000 available in 1982, it would be possible to retire safely at age sixty. The recommended distribution of funds would be about $50,000 in dividend stock at 8 percent for $4000 the first year, and $100,000 in bonds returning about $12,000 per year, and $50,000 in capital appreciation stocks returning $10,000 per year. These sums plus retirement pension and extra income, and eventually Social Security, would permit the accumulation of additional capital through the early retirement years.

In summary, then, you can begin planning for retirement at any time by using current financial data to calculate what would happen under several different scenarios.

Appendix A

MY RESERVOIR OF STOCKS

Following is a list of the stocks that are presently in my reservoir and that have been there for many years.

AMERICAN STOCK EXCHANGE

NAME	SYMBOL	BUSINESS
AAV Companies	AAV	vending
Altamil	ALW	trucking, hardware
Blessings Corp.	BCO	diaper service
Bro-Dart	BD	supplier of library products
Brooks and Perkins	BPI	air cargo handling equipment
Buell Industries	BUE	custom-engineered fasteners
Buildex, Inc.	BLX	architectural and hardware components
Carolina Energies	CEI	gas utility
CDI Corp.	CDI	engineering service company
Cellu-Craft	CC	packaging material and linen service
Chadwick-Miller	CWK	distributor of low-cost houseware and gifts
CHB Foods	CBF	canner of fish products
Clausing Corp.	CLA	metal-cutting tools
CMI Corp.	CMX	road-building equipment
Commercial Metals	CMC	metal trader and processor

NAME	SYMBOL	BUSINESS
Condec Corp.	CDT	valves and heavy equipment
Conroy, Inc.	CRY	pleasure boats
Consolidated Refining	CDR	fabricator of precision metals
Crompton Co.	CRC	corduroy and velveteen
Crown Crafts	CRW	velvet and suede
Del Laboratories	DLI	drugs, cosmetics, and toiletries
Digicon, Inc.	DGC	geophysical services
Downey Savings & Loan	DSL	savings and loan
Drug Fair	DF	discount drug stores
Eastern Company	EML	mine roof support
Edmos Corp.	EDM	double-knit textiles
Esquire Radio & Electronics	EE	electronics, hardware, entertainment equipment
Evans Aristocrat	EVS	measuring devices and leather goods
Fab Industries	FIT	warp-knit textiles
Fisher and Porter	FP	process controls and water treatment systems
Frantz Manufacturing	FRZ	garage doors
General Houseware	GHW	cookware, leisure furniture, gifts
Glasrock Medical Services	GLA	plastic and ceramic products
Gorman-Rupp	GRC	pumps
Grand Auto	GAI	automobile parts retail stores

NAME	SYMBOL	BUSINESS
Great American Ind.	GRI	rubber products, sports equipment
Hasting Manufacturing	HMF	automotive replacement parts
Hipotronics	HIP	high voltage test equipment
Howell Industries	HOW	automotive equipment, windshields
ICH, Corp.	ICH	holding company, life insurance
IMC Magnetics	IMG	airmovers, motors, hydraulic compressors
International Seaway Trading	INS	footwear importer
Jaclyn	JLN	handbags
Jensen	JI	products for recreational vehicles and construction
Jupiter Industries	JUP	trucking natural gas distributor
Ketchum & Co.	KCH	distributor of drugs and health supplies
La Barge, Inc.	LB	tubular steel fabrication, electronics
La Maur	LMR	grooming products
La Pointe	LPI	electronics products
Lodge & Shipley	LSP	machine tools
LSB Industries	LSB	machine tools, bearings, air conditioning
Lehigh Press	LP	commercial printer
Maine Public Service	MAP	electric power distributor
Maul Technology	MTY	gearings, plating, glass
Means (F.W.) and Co.	MNS	linen rental service

NAME	SYMBOL	BUSINESS
Michigan General	MGL	diversified
Mite Corporation	MTE	industrial products
Movie Star	MVSA	lingerie and lounge wear
OEA, Inc.	OEA	propellant and electro-explosive devices
Pat Fashions	PI	apparel importer
Penn Engineering & Mfg.	PNN	fastening devices
Pennsylvania Engr.	PEC	support for steel industries
Pep Boys	PBY	retail automotive sales
Pratt and Lambert	PM	paints
Pratt-Read	PRA	piano keyboards, screwdriver blades
Providence Gas	PVY	natural gas distributor
Prudential Bldg. Maint.	PBM	maintenance services
Raymond Industries	RAE	military aerospace and oil well services
Russell Corp.	RML	athletic uniforms, leisurewear
Schenuit Industries	SCH	home lawn and garden products
SGL Industries	SL	diversified
Shelter Resources	SHL	mobile homes
Sierracin Corp.	SER	impact-resistant windows
SMD Industries	SDI	rack manufacturer
Spencer Companies	SPN	women's apparel and shoes
SSP Industries	SSS	aerospace, agricultural, construction equipment

NAME	SYMBOL	BUSINESS
Standard Products	SPD	rubber and plastic parts, tracks for tanks
Stephan Chemical	SCL	specialty chemicals
United Aircraft Products	UAP	heat exchanges
Universal Cigars	UCG	cigars
Vernition	VRN	medical equipment
Vishay Intertechnology	VSH	precision resistors
Vulcan Corporation	VUL	shoe components, bowling pins
Wellco	WLC	boots, casual shoes
Work Wear	WKW	garment manufacturing and rental

NEW YORK STOCK EXCHANGE

NAME	SYMBOL	BUSINESS
American Hoist & Derrick	AHO	heavy lifting equipment
American Standard	AST	plumbing
Apache Corp.	APA	oil and gas exploration
APL Corp.	APL	paper products
Armada	ABW	electrical resistance alloys, rendering
Arrow Electronics	ARW	distributor
Avco	AV	consumer financing, life insurance, movies
Banner Industries	BNR	trucking, industrial products
Bell Industries	BI	electronic products
Bemis Co.	BMS	packaging items and equipment

NAME	SYMBOL	BUSINESS
Bobbie Brooks	BBK	apparel
Borden, Inc.	BN	food, dairy products
Brockway Glass	BRK	glass containers
Bundy Corp.	BNY	small diameter tubing
Butler International	BTL	specialized trucking
Cabot Corp.	CBT	carbon black
Carter Wallace	CAR	drugs, deodorants, shaving cream
Clark Equipment	CKL	lift trucks, heavy duty trucks
CTS Corp.	CTS	variable resistors
Culbro Corp.	CUC	cigars
Damon Corp.	DMN	medical instruments, clinical labs
Daniel Industries	DAN	systems for measuring flow of oil and gas
Dayco	DAY	plastics and consumer products
Dorsey Corp.	DSY	glass and plastic containers
Dynamic Corp. of America	DYA	consumer electrical houseware
Eagle-Pisher	EPI	diversified
Easco	ES	hand tools
Eastern Air Lines	EAL	airlines
Esquire	ESQ	educational materials
Federal Paper Board	FBO	paper board, pulp, boxboard, cartons
Federal Signal	FSS	signaling devices

NAME	SYMBOL	BUSINESS
Ford Motor	F	automobiles
Gearhart Industries	GOI	oil well digging service and equipment
General Motors	GM	automobiles
Giddings & Lewis	GID	machine tools
Gould, Inc.	GLD	batteries & electrical products
Great Lakes International	GL	dredging
Gulf & Western Ind.	GW	diversified
Helmerich & Payne	HP	off-shore drilling
Hoover Universal	HVU	diversified
IBM Corp.	IBM	computers
Ideal Toy	ID	toys
Jorgensen (Earle M.)	JOR	steel and aluminum distributor
Katy Ind.	KT	diversified
Keller Ind.	KEL	aluminum products for the home
Keystone Consolidated	KES	steel, wire, hardware products
Lamson & Sessions	LMS	industrial fasteners, freight car doors
McNeil Corp.	MME	industrial equipment
Napco	NAP	distributor
Norlin Corp.	NRL	musical instruments, brewery
Overhead Doors	OHD	garage doors
Palm Beach	PMB	men's apparel
Public Service of Colorado	PSR	electric-gas utility

NAME	SYMBOL	BUSINESS
Quanex Corp.	NX	tubing
Rowan Companies	RDC	on- and off-shore drilling
Savin Corp.	SVB	copy machines
SCA Services	SCV	waste service
Selegman & Latz	SAL	beauty salons
Shapell Industries	SHA	home builder
Singer Co.	SMF	sewing machines
Soo Line	SOO	railroad
Southdown, Inc.	SDW	cement, oil and gas
Steego	STG	distributor of automobile equipment
Stone Container	STO	containers, paper board
Tandy	TAN	retailer, electrical products
Teledyne	TDY	engines, machine tools, diversified
Tracor	TRR	electronics
Tyco Laboratories	TYC	fire sprinkler devices, cable, solar cells
UNR Ind.	UNR	railroad car components, tubing, diversified
U.S. Industries	USI	diversified
Varo	VRO	night viewing systems
Vulcan, Inc.	VX	ingot molds and castings
Westinghouse Electric	WX	electrical equipment

Following is a list of recent additions to my reservoir.

AMERICAN STOCK EXCHANGE		
NAME	SYMBOL	BUSINESS
Arrow Automotive Ind.	AI	replacement parts
Barco of California	BRC	uniforms
Big V Supermarkets	BIV	supermarkets
Billy the Kid	BTK	boys' wear
Bowl America	BWL	operator of bowling alleys
Branch Ind.	BII	trucking
Burgess Ind.	BGS	environmental controls
Campbell Resources	CCH	mining, oil and gas
Cetec Corp	CEC	electronics, plastics
Clark Cons. Ind.	CLK	electronic supplies
Clopay	CPY	overhead doors, home products
Compo	CEM	leather substitutes
CompuDyne Corp.	CDC	visual communication
Concord Fabrics	CIS	woven and knitted fabrics
Crest-Foam	CFO	foam
C.S. Group	CSG	women's sportswear
Decorator Ind.	DII	draperies
Diodes, Inc.	DIO	semiconductors
DWG Corp.	DWG	distributor of gas
EAC Ind.	EAC	home security, hardware
Empire of Carolina	EMP	toys
Frisch's Restaurants	FRS	Big Boy's restaurants
Galaxy Carpet Mills	GXY	carpets

Garan	GAN	men's and children's apparel
Genovese Drugstores	GDX	drug stores
Hampton Ind.	HAI	apparel
Hasbro	HAS	toys and games
Hofmann Ind.	HOF	steel tubing
IFS Ind.	IFN	funeral services
Imperial Ind.	III	building products
International Proteins	PRO	fishmeal, shrimp
Jetronic Ind.	JET	furniture distributor, electronics
Kinark	KIN	specialty chemicals, hotels
Liberty Fabrics	LBY	lace
Lynch Corp.	LGL	quartz crystals
Medalist Ind.	MDI	leisure products
MEM Co.	MEM	toiletries
Movielab, Inc.	MOV	motion picture film processor
National Patent Development	NPD	medical and optical products
Nichols (S.E.)	NCL	discount department stores
Noel Ind.	NOL	jeans
Nolex	NLX	distributor of printing paper
Ohio Art Co.	OAR	toys
Ohio-Sealy Mattress	OMT	mattresses
Perry Drugstores	PDS	drugstores
Pioneer Systems	PAE	parachutes, craft items

Ply-Gem Ind.	PGI	plywood
Ravin Ind.	RAV	insulated garments
Refrigerated Transport	REF	trucking
Republic Gypsum	RGC	gypsum board
Restaurant Associates	RA	food and newsstands
Riblet Prod.	RIB	products for housing
RSC Ind.	RSC	wire products
Servisco	SVO	work clothing, building maintenance
Sorg Paper	SOG	paper
Stanwood Corp.	SNW	men's and boys' apparel
Superior Surgical Mfg.	SGC	uniforms
System Planning Corp.	SPZ	engineering services
Technitrol, Inc.	TNL	electronic products
Three D Departments	TDD	operates drapery departments
Tidwell Ind.	TWI	mobile homes
U.N.A Corp.	UNA	steel importer
Valspar Corp.	VAL	paint
Verit Ind.	VER	meat processing
Vertipile, Inc.	VRT	flock-coated materials
Willcox and Gibbs	WG	equipment for apparel manufacturing

NEW YORK STOCK EXCHANGE

NAME	SYMBOL	BUSINESS
Anthony Ind.	ANT	swimming pools
Arkansas Best	ABZ	trucking
AVX Corp.	AVX	capacitors
Belding Heminway	BHY	specialty thread
Borman's Inc.	BRF	supermarkets
Cadence Ind.	CDE	comic books
Carolina Freight Carriers	COA	trucking
Cascade Natural Gas	CGC	gas distributor
Champion Spark Plugs	CHM	spark plugs
Chelsea Ind.	CDD	shoe products
Chock Full O'Nuts	CHF	restaurants
Clorox Co.	CLX	bleach
Cluett, Peabody	CLU	apparel
Coleco Ind.	CLO	toys
Colgate-Palmolive	CL	household products
Collins and Aikman	CK	fabrics
Dan River	DML	textiles
Diversified Ind.	DMC	metal processing, castings
Elixir Ind.	EXR	diversified
Fabric Centers of Amer.	FCA	chain of fabric stores
Fox-Stanley Photo Prod.	FSP	photo finisher

Graniteville Co.	GVL	apparel, fabric
Hart Schaffner & Marx	HSM	men's clothing
Ludlow Corp.	LUD	packaging
National Homes	NHX	panellized homes
National Tea	NTY	supermarkets
Newell Co.	NWL	drapery hardware
Pueblo International	PII	supermarkets
Puerto Rican Cement	PRN	cement
Redman Ind.	RE	mobile homes
Reece Corp.	RCE	button hole machinery
Saga Corp.	SGA	restaurants
Scott Lad Foods	SLF	supermarkets
Tootsie Roll Ind.	TR	candy
Triangle Ind.	TRI	wire and cable
UMET Trust	UAT	business trust
Union Corp.	UCO	diversified
United Brands	UB	bananas
Universal Foods	UFC	cheese, gourmet foods
Warner-Lambert	WLA	drugs

Appendix B
SUGGESTED READING

The following books are recommended as background reading for the small investor.

Amling, Frederick. *Investments: An Introduction to Analysis and Management.* 4th ed. Englewood Cliffs, New Jersey: Prentice-Hall, 1978.

Bailard, Thomas E., et al. *Personal Money Management.* 3rd ed. Chicago, Illinois: SRA, 1979.

Leffler, G. L. and Farwell, L. C. *The Stock Market.* 3rd ed. New York: Ronald Press, 1963.

Mills, Ronald K. *Successful Investing.* New York: Simon & Schuster, 1979.

Randle, Paul A. and Swensen, Philip R. *Personal Financial Planning for Executives.* Belmont, California: Lifetime Learning Publications, 1981.

________. *Financial Planning for the Physician and Dentist.* Belmont, California: Lifetime Learning Publications, 1982.

Rosenberg, Claude N., Jr. *Stock Market Primer.* New York: Warner Books, 1970.

INDEX